JOHN KNOX

JOHN KNOX

John J. Murray

 PUBLISHING WITH A MISSION

EP BOOKS
Faverdale North
Darlington, DL3 0PH, England

web: http://www.epbooks.org
e-mail: sales@epbooks.org

133 North Hanover Street
Carlisle, PA 17013, USA

www.epbooks.us
e-mail: usasales@epbooks.org

First published 2011

British Library Cataloguing in Publication Data available

ISBN-13: 978-0-85234-759-1   ISBN-10: 0-85234-759-6

Printed and bound in Great Britain by the MPG Books Group

To

WILLIAM H. MURRAY
a beloved brother
and a faithful supporter
in literature ministry

Statue of John Knox, New College, Edinburgh

CONTENTS

PREFACE

The year 2010 marked the 450th anniversary of the Scottish Reformation, and I was invited to write a short commemorative history of the event. In taking a fresh look at the Reformation story my appreciation of the part played by John Knox was greatly increased. It was therefore a delight for me to respond to the request to contribute a short account of his life for this series of bitesize biographies. I hope this introduction to John Knox will stimulate greater interest in the Reformer and especially in the light of the commemoration of the 500th anniversary of his birth, 2014.

I would like to express my sincere thanks to Mr Maurice Grant for his assistance in checking the original manuscript, and also to the series editor, Dr Michael Haykin, for valuable suggestions.

JOHN J. MURRAY
September 2011

Knox timeline

1551   Appointed preacher in St Nicholas Church, Newcastle; appointed chaplain to Edward VI

1553   Itinerant preacher in the South of England; Mary Tudor becomes Queen of England

1554   Knox seeks refuge on the Continent; arrives in Geneva; appointed minister in Frankfurt

1555   Leaves Frankfurt for Geneva; returns to Scotland; marries Marjory Bowes

1556   Returns to Geneva as minister of English congregation there

1557   First Covenant (the Godly Band) drawn up by the Lords of the Congregation

1558   Martyrdom of Walter Mill; Mary Tudor (Mary I) dies; succeeded by Elizabeth I; Protestant exiles return home

1559   Knox in Dieppe for two months; arrives in Leith; appointed minister at St Giles

1560   Mary of Guise dies; Treaty of Edinburgh; States of Scotland agree suppression of Romanism; *Scots Confession* approved; *Book of Discipline* drawn up; The Geneva Bible published; his wife Marjory dies; First General Assembly of the Reformed Church

1561   Mary, Queen of Scots, arrives in Edinburgh

1564   Knox marries Margaret Stewart

1567   Mary surrenders throne to her son James Stewart (James VI of Scotland and James I of England); Earl of Moray appointed Regent

1570   Moray assassinated and succeeded by the Earl of Lennox

1571   Knox forced to leave for St Andrews; Lennox dies and succeeded by Earl of Mar

1572   Knox returns to Edinburgh; Mar dies and succeeded by the Earl of Morton; Knox dies in his home at the age of fifty-eight

1578   *Second Book of Discipline*

1

THE BACKGROUND:

'Wherefore was Master Patrick burned?'

On 29 February 1528, a young man of twenty-four years was burnt alive at the stake outside St Salvator's College in St Andrews. He was Patrick Hamilton, born of noble parentage and on his mother's side related to King James V of Scotland. He was appointed titular Abbot of Fearn at the age of thirteen. Later he went to the University of Paris and then to the University of St Andrews where he was most likely taught by John Major. He became a priest probably in 1526. How could such a person be executed by the authorities in the very church in which he had been raised?

The explanation is that he had embraced what the Church of his day regarded as dangerous heresy. The Medieval Roman Catholic Church, with the pope as its head, had held sway in Europe for centuries. But the Christianity it represented bore little resemblance to that of the New Testament church. It was about the fourth century AD that things began to change, after which there was a gradual deformation of Christianity. The visible presence of God's true church all but disappeared from western Christendom, limiting it to small pockets of the authentic apostolic gospel that persisted — the Waldensians in Italy, the Hussites in Bohemia and the Lollards in England, for example.

During that time the human authority of the pope and the fallible teaching of the Church replaced the unique authority of God in the Scriptures. Man's works had taken the place of the sovereign and irresistible grace of God in salvation. The result of such apostasy was idolatry, typified by the cult of Mary and of the saints, the worship of the Eucharist, the pseudo-magical power of the priests in the use of the sacraments, the efficacy of relics and so on. John Calvin's view was that at the very centre of the Roman Church was a form of Christianized idolatry.

The country of Scotland, although on the edge of Europe, was not immune from the influences of Rome. Yet it did have the light of the gospel for a few centuries, brought by missionaries such as Ninian in the Whithorn area of the south-west. The real and effective evangelization of Scotland began with Columba, who emigrated from Ireland to Argyll, accompanied by his disciples, in AD 563, and set up his base in the island of Iona. The Celtic Church, to which he belonged, was Bible-centred and missionary-minded. It spread its influence into England and it is said that the mission stemming from Iona extended itself in a generation or so 'from the shores of the Forth to the banks of the Thames'. It was an autonomous self-governing body of Christian people.

The Roman mission came to Britain through Augustine of Canterbury. He was sent by Gregory the Great in 596 to convert the 'pagan' English. There were differences of ethos and observance between the Church founded by

Augustine and the Celtic Church. At the Synod of Whitby in 664 judgement was given in favour of the Roman Church, thus bringing what would be the British Isles within the mainstream of Christendom. As the influence of the Celtic Church waned, so the Roman Church influence increased in Scotland. The further Romanizing of the Church was carried forward by Queen Margaret (c. 1047–93), wife of Malcolm Canmore, who influenced the Scottish court in an English direction and the Church in a Roman one. Their son David lavished much wealth on the bishoprics and monasteries he founded.

By the beginning of the sixteenth century the Medieval Church had a stranglehold upon Scotland, and had acquired absolute authority over the souls of men and women. Amid a population of relatively poor people, it owned the finest buildings in the land. It is estimated that, owning more than half the real estate in the country, it received an annual income of some £400,000, in contrast to the meagre £40,000 of the Crown. These revenues were partially derived from the lands of the nobles and wealthy merchants, and partially from tithes and other ecclesiastical dues. The pope, the king, the nobles and, in certain cases within their dioceses, the bishops, all claimed the right to make appointments to benefices. The pope claimed the lion's share and this caused intense discontent.

At that time there were more than 1,000 churches in Scotland, but of those over 900 were appropriated to monasteries, cathedrals and collegiate churches, which either drew the revenues or farmed them out. In a country where the population was only around 800,000, priests numbered perhaps as many as 3,000. Some priests, it appeared, could scarcely say the alphabet, and there were those who could not read their own language without stammering. According to George Buchanan, many of them were so ignorant of the Scriptures that they believed the New Testament was a recent book written by Martin Luther (1483–1546).

It is not surprising, therefore, to discover the ignorance among the laity. The Latin Vulgate was the Bible of the Church for over a millennium and no interpretation of it was to be given contrary to the teaching of the Church. The church services were conducted in Latin. The possession or study of the Scriptures in the common tongue frequently invoked a charge of heresy. Few of the ordinary people could read anyway.

It was at the same time a Church steeped in moral decay. In spite of a profession of chastity on the part of each clergyman, there was rampant immorality in the Church. Cardinal David Beaton, the Archbishop of St Andrews, had about eleven illegitimate children. There were seventeen bishops at the time of the Reformation, of whom twelve had illegitimate children. And many of the abbots, themselves the illegitimate offspring of the king or nobles, also had plenty of their own. Sons of such liaisons were given lucrative positions in the Church, and daughters married into the nobility. In 1552 a Roman Catholic Catechism was prepared by order of the Archbishop of St Andrews, John Hamilton (c.1511–1571), with the object of instructing the people in the Ten Commandments, the Creed, the sacraments and the Lord's Prayer. It represented a high code of morality. The Catholic 'reformation' focused on practical moral abuses — it did not seek to reform the theology of the Church.

Martin Luther is considered 'the father of the Protestant Reformation'. A Roman Catholic friar, as he agonized over the state of his soul, he came to experience the New Testament doctrine of 'justification by faith alone'. This revolutionized his life and he began to expose the corruptions of Rome, especially the abuse of 'Indulgences' whereby the remission of punishment in purgatory could be bought with money. The public exposure came with the nailing of the *Ninety-Five Theses* to the church door at Wittenberg on 31 October 1517, giving birth to the Protestant Reformation.

Patrick Hamilton had been brought into contact with the teaching of Luther in Paris and later on in Marburg. It was there that he wrote a set of *Theses*, distinctly Lutheran articles of faith, which were later translated into English by John Firth and published under the title *Patrick's Places*. When Patrick Hamilton began to preach these doctrines with great boldness the clergy were alarmed, especially Cardinal Beaton. If the new teaching prevailed, then the absolute authority of the church over the souls of men would be at an end. He was moving the whole basis of salvation from the church to Christ. When it became apparent that Hamilton would not give up his beliefs he was condemned as a heretic. He died proclaiming: 'It is for the truth of God for which I now suffer.' His last words were: 'How long, O Lord, shall darkness overwhelm this realm? How long will you suffer this tyranny of men? Lord Jesus, receive my spirit.'

By their action against Hamilton the authorities thought that the reforming movement would be suppressed. In their joy at the burning of such a notable heretic, the popish clergy and professors of the University of Louvain wrote a letter dated 21 April 1528, which congratulated their companions in Scotland. But it did not help their cause as it made the people question the circumstances of Hamilton's death and take an interest in the theology he had espoused. Archbishop

Beaton was advised to burn other heretics in deep cellars 'for the reek [smoke] of Patrick Hamilton has infected all it blew upon'. In his *History of the Reformation* John Knox notes that after Master Patrick's death 'the knowledge of God did wondrously increase within this realm, partly by reading, partly by brotherly conference ... but chiefly by merchants and mariners', and that within the whole realm there were few hearing of Hamilton's death who did not begin to enquire: 'Wherefore was Master Patrick burned?'

It was probably a year after the martyrdom of Hamilton that a young man appeared in St Andrews to study at St Salvator's College. His name was John Knox — a man destined to carry forward the work of reformation begun by Hamilton.

2

THE EARLY YEARS:

'One is sufficient for a sacrifice'

John Knox was born about the year 1514 at Giffordgate in the East Lothian market town of Haddington. It was one of the leading towns of the county. Close to the River Tyne, which flows through it, is St Mary's, the largest parish church in Scotland, called the 'Lamp of Lothian'. John's father William was a merchant or craftsman in Haddington; his mother was a Sinclair of Northrig, perhaps with a sister married to George Ker of Samuelston, three miles south of the town. Whatever the status of William Knox, he was able to set up his eldest son William in business and send John to the schools. It is likely that John attended Haddington Grammar School, and from there he went to St Andrews University to study at St Salvator's College.

It was just outside the archway leading to St Salvator's College that young Patrick Hamilton had been burnt at the stake for heresy. If Knox had not already encountered the new teaching for which Hamilton had lost his life, he must have heard about it from his fellow students. A century and a half earlier, followers of the English Reformer, John Wycliff, had settled in Kyle, Ayrshire. Wycliff had openly attacked the abuses in the Church and urged people to read the Bible for themselves. His followers were called 'Lollards'. The teaching spread and a Lollard named James Resby was burned as a heretic in Perth in 1407, and in 1433 Paul Craw, a Bohemian student at St Andrews University, was arrested and burned at the stake because he was a follower of John Huss, a Bohemian Reformer influenced by Wycliff.

It is almost certain that Knox studied theology with the internationally famous scholar John Major, graduate of Cambridge and Paris, and Professor at the Sorbonne. Major was critical of the abuses of the Church and under him a young student would be constrained to take a critical look at the ecclesiastical and political establishment. Since we do not know the exact date of Knox's graduation we cannot say precisely when he left university. His activities during the late 1530s are unknown, although it appears that he had been ordained to the priesthood as early as 1536. By 1540 he appears as a notary apostolic in East Lothian. He was actually appointed on papal authority and represented clients in church courts. Much of the notary work was done in private houses, drawing up title deeds, marriage contracts and wills, and sorting out financial disputes. He was based at Samuelston, possibly living with his mother's relatives.

In fact it was on 13 December 1540 that Knox first entered the written records, appearing that day at Haddington market cross on behalf of a James Ker of Samuelston. When his name appears in the records again in 1543 he was living in Ker's house and acting as a tutor. In the last extant document that he notarized, dated 17 March 1543, one finds an interesting attestation: *Testis per Christum fidelis, cui gloria* (a faithful witness to Christ, to whom be the glory). These words may indicate that he had by then become a Protestant. It was in that same year that the Bible was allowed to be used in Scotland.

Like John Calvin, Knox was very reticent in speaking of his spiritual experiences and we have only hints as to how the great change came about in his life. In one place he says, 'It pleased God to call me from the puddle of Papistry.' Disgusted with what he saw of the corruption of the Church he would have spent time in studying the Bible. On his deathbed Knox asked his wife to read to him the seventeenth chapter of John's Gospel, where he said, 'I first cast my anchor.' There is no doubt that Knox would have encountered the new Protestant teaching at St Andrews University. Lutheran writings and tracts by the Swiss Reformers had been circulating throughout the Continent. By 1525 and again in 1535 statutes had been passed forbidding the importation of Lutheran books or the teaching of Lutheran doctrines. Knox points out that merchants and mariners who encountered the new views in Europe propagated them on their return to Scotland. Scholars who studied in Germany did the same thing in St Andrews and the other Scottish universities. Cardinal Beaton testified in the 1530s that the Lutheran 'heresy' was increasing apace.

Further measures were taken in 1540 against those who held heretical views. Among them the most revealing was that forbidding 'private conventicles'. These prayer meetings and Bible study groups, later known as 'Privy Kirks', were established on the French pattern and they greatly assisted the spread of Protestantism. Quite a number of the nobility opposed the persecution for they had turned Protestant or were inclined that way. The King, James V, remained firm in his allegiance to the pope and to the Roman Catholic Church. He strengthened Scotland's traditional alliance with Roman Catholic France by marrying Princess Madeleine, daughter of the French king. When she died he replaced her with a handsome French aristocratic widow, Mary of Guise. Relations with England and his uncle Henry VIII, who had already broken with Rome, were deteriorating. James V, influenced by his clerics, decided to take direct action to forestall any English attack by invading England himself. The outcome was the disaster of Solway Moss in November 1542, where a Scottish army of 10,000, mishandled and misled, was defeated by an English force about one-fifth its size. James V, literally willing himself to death, passed away at the age of thirty, leaving as his heir to the throne the six-day-old Mary (later to become Mary, Queen of Scots).

Following this event James Hamilton, Earl of Arran, was appointed Regent. He was regarded as being favourable to Protestantism, if he had not already accepted it. He began by appointing as his chaplains two Protestant preachers: Thomas Guilliame, a former Black Friar, and John Rough — both of whom were to have a great influence upon Knox. According to the historian David Calderwood, Guilliame was 'the first man from whom Mr Knox received any taste of the truth'. Having heard both men preach, Knox said of Guilliame, 'his doctrine was wholesome without great vehemence against superstition'. He liked Rough better for he was 'more simple and more vehement against all impiety'. The Regent felt that the eventual unification of the English and Scottish crowns was the only possible solution to many of Scotland's problems. With the approval of Parliament he sent a delegation to England to discuss the possible marriage of the English heir, Prince Edward, to Mary, Queen of Scots.

The outcome was the Treaty of Greenwich, duly concluded on 1 July 1543 and ratified by the Regent Arran in August.

Protestantism seemed to be further strengthened when Parliament granted permission in 1543 for the proposal to make the Old and New Testaments in the vernacular legal, as long as people did not dispute about them. However, there were other forces at work. The Queen Mother, Mary of Guise, had a strong influence on affairs, along with Cardinal David Beaton. The coronation of the young Queen Mary in September 1543 was quickly followed by confirmation of the 'auld alliance' with France. It was the Protestants' turn to be apprehensive. To arrest the spread of heresy, all Protestants, including Arran's chaplains, along with such advisers as James Kirkcaldy of Grange, Henry Balnaves, Thomas Ballantyne and Sir David Lindsay of the Mount, were ousted from their positions and persecution began once again. It would soon come near to John Knox himself.

The area of Lothian where he lived was becoming a hotbed of those who favoured drastic reform within the Church. By 1540 a group of lairds had become Protestant and within three years were actively supporting the idea of a close Anglo-Scottish alliance. By this time Knox had moved from Samuelston to Longniddry to become tutor to Francis and George, the two sons of Hugh Douglas of Longniddry, and Alexander, the eldest son of Cockburn of Ormiston. Hugh Douglas had his own private chapel and the local people came to listen when Knox catechized the boys and instructed them in the Bible. He was in effect no longer a priest but a Protestant teacher.

At this point George Wishart appeared on the scene. It would be part of Wishart's work to bring the disparate Protestant groups into closer contact with each other, and by his eventual martyrdom to provide them with a common cause. He was also destined to have a profound effect on Knox in bringing him to take a militant public stand for the new teaching. Wishart was about the same age as Knox, born around 1513 in Angus. He was a student at Louvain where he graduated in arts in 1532. He was a schoolmaster in Montrose but was pursued by the Bishop of Brechin when he fled the country in 1538. He was for a time in England and then went back to the Continent. On his return in 1543 he ministered in Montrose and expounded the Scriptures to all who showed interest. He embarked on preaching tours that took him to Dundee, Fife, Ayrshire and East Lothian, and he was under threat for his teaching from Cardinal David Beaton, Archbishop of St Andrews.

While in East Lothian he was guarded by a band of friends and admirers, among them John Knox. It was usually Knox who carried a large two-handed sword before Wishart. The young Reformer went to preach in St Mary's, Haddington. In his final sermon there Wishart warned the people what a fearful fate awaited them if they ignored the Word of God. When he finished the sermon he went over and said goodbye to his followers. He was to spend that night at the house of the Laird of Ormiston. Knox was prepared to accompany him but Wishart stopped him with the words: 'Nay, return you to your bairns [pupils] and God bless you. One is sufficient for a sacrifice.'

Later that night Wishart was seized by the Earl of Bothwell, who promised safe keeping but later broke the promise and handed him over to Cardinal Beaton, who imprisoned him in his castle. On 1 March 1546 Wishart was tried by an ecclesiastical court at which Beaton presided. Wishart said that he had taught only what was in the Scriptures,

but his protests were to no avail. The Cardinal pronounced
the death sentence. The next day Wishart was taken to the
stake at the east part of the castle, where his hands were
tied behind his back, a noose was placed round his neck,
and an iron chain fastened round his waist. His pockets and
sleeves were stuffed with small bags of gunpowder. Fearing
an attempt to rescue him, the Cardinal had his castle guns
trained on the place of execution. Wishart knelt down to
pray and made his final speech in which he said,

> For this cause I am sent, that I should suffer this fire for
> Christ's sake. Consider and behold my visage, ye shall not see
> me change my colour. This grim fire I fear not.

As he died in the flames, Cardinal Beaton watched in
satisfaction.

Wishart's preaching helped to popularize the teaching
of the Swiss Reformers in Scotland. He had translated into
English the first *Helvetic Confession of Faith* of 1536. He
argued that the true church is known by faithful preaching of
the Word and the lawful administration of the sacraments. It
is believed that he observed the first Communion in Scotland
according to the rediscovered New Testament teaching. His
life and teaching had a deep and lasting effect on Knox. As
one reads Knox's account of Wishart's last weeks in Lothian
one cannot but feel he is almost thinking in terms of Elijah's
commissioning of Elisha to take up the prophetic task after
him. Knox had taken his stand for the gospel and would not
look back.

3

ST ANDREWS:

'where God opened my mouth to his glory'

It is not surprising that Wishart's cruel death aroused anger against Cardinal David Beaton. On 29 May 1546 a small band of nobles from Fife entered the castle at St Andrews via the drawbridge, aroused the Cardinal from his bed and confronted him with drawn swords. James Melville, pointing his sword at Beaton, declared:

> Repent thee of thy former wicked life, and especially the shedding of the blood of that notable instrument of God, Master George Wishart, which albeit the flame of fire consumed before men, yet cries out a vengeance upon thee, and we from God are sent to revenge it.

Beaton's last words, according to Knox, were: 'I am a priest, I am a priest, fye, fye, all is gone.' It is true in a sense that the old Church regime and the French alliance were doomed, and all that, says A. R. MacEwan, 'before Knox had preached a single sermon'. But the sermon was soon to follow.

The assassins who had forced their way into the castle to commit the deed considered that the best course of action was to hold the castle, which was well fortified and well supplied. Before long, others joined them in the defence of the castle, including Sir James Kirkcaldy of Grange and John Rough, one of the two chaplains of Regent Arran, when he was leaning towards Protestantism. In all, there were between 120 and 150 men in the garrison. Arran made plans to besiege the castle but with the Castilians (for such they came to be called) well supplied with munitions and food the siege got nowhere. They begged Henry VIII of England to send an army to help them. Eventually the siege was suspended and there was an agreement reached to hold the castle for the Regent and not to hand it over to the English. The truce lasted from January to June 1547. During that period the occupants were permitted to come and go.

Following the death of Wishart, Knox continued his duties as tutor. Since he had become known as one of Wishart's followers he could be sure that the ecclesiastical authorities would be hot on his trail to make him recant, or else. Tired of having to be on the move, Knox considered leaving for the Continent. The noblemen, Douglas of Longniddry and Cockburn of Ormiston, whose sons he was tutoring, advised him to take his three charges to St Andrews Castle. Knox accepted their advice and on 10 April 1547 he arrived at the castle with pupils Francis and George Douglas, and Alexander Cockburn.

It was in the castle at St Andrews that Knox's real life work began. As was his practice in Longniddry he continued to instruct the three boys in grammar, the classics and theology. At the same time he also read to them a catechism of which they had to give an account publicly in the parish

Kirk. He lectured to them on the Gospel of John in the chapel within the castle. A large number of people gathered to hear the instruction, including John Rough, now the preacher to the garrison, and Henry Balnaves of Halhill, graduate of St Andrews, judge and former ambassador. Both were impressed with Knox's abilities and urged him to become Rough's colleague in the preaching. Knox refused at first, alleging 'that he could not run where God had not called him'.

Rough and Balnaves were not prepared to accept his refusal and, after seeking advice, decided that he should be called to the office of minister publicly, so that he would have no conscientious grounds for refusing. The next time that Rough preached in the castle he addressed the question of how preachers were chosen, underlining the power of the congregation to select a suitable candidate. Turning to Knox he declared:

> Brother, ye shall not be offended, albeit that I speak unto you that which I have in charge, even from all those who are here present, which is this. In the name of God and his Son Jesus Christ, and in the name of those that presently calls you by mouth, I charge you that you refuse not his holy vocation.

Turning to the congregation he said, 'Was this not your charge to me?' and 'Do you not approve this vocation?' With the response from the people being positive it was all too much for Knox and his immediate reaction was neither to accept nor reject but to break into tears and leave the chapel. After several days, in which he kept to himself, he agreed to answer the call.

His first sermon was in the parish church in St Andrews at a service attended by the faculty of St Andrews University

and a large number of the clergy. He took as his text Daniel
7:24-25, concerning the little horn or kingdom which would
arise after the ten horns or kingdoms had grown from the
head of the fourth apocalyptic beast. In the course of his
sermon he maintained that the Roman Church, which had
arisen out of the wreckage of the Roman Empire, was the
Antichrist spoken of in the New Testament. He then went
on to deal with the lives of various popes, and the teaching
of the Roman Church that conflicted with the doctrine of
justification by faith alone. He ended by saying that if anyone
present disagreed with his interpretation of Scripture he
would discuss the matter afterwards and show that the
things he taught were in accordance with the truth. The
sermon created a sensation. Some said, 'Others sned [lop
off] the branches of the papistry, but he strikes at the root
also, to destroy the whole.' Others declared: 'Master George
Wishart never spoke so plainly; and yet he was burnt. Even
so will John Knox be.'

Opposition came from the Black and Grey Friars. The
outcome was a public debate in St Leonard's yard at the
university. This confrontation took place before Dean John
Winram, who had been reprimanded for allowing Knox to
preach his sermon in the parish church without at the same
time opposing his teaching. Nine articles were prepared,
setting forth the doctrine put forward by the Protestants.
They contained a denial of the pope as head of the church,
terming him Antichrist, and a rejection of any religion not
based exclusively on the Bible, declaring the Mass to be
an abomination, purgatory non-existent and prayers for
the dead vanity and idolatry. First Rough and then Knox
were called to acknowledge these as their beliefs. Dialogue
then commenced and Winram raised the question of the

lawfulness of ceremonies being added to those required by the Scriptures. Knox's response was clear: 'Man may neither make or devise a religion that is acceptable to God: but man is bound to observe and keep the religion that from God is received, without chopping or changing thereof.'

Again, he said, 'That God's word damns your ceremonies, it is evident; for the plain and straight commandment of God is, Not that thing which appears good in thine eyes, shalt thou do to the Lord thy God, but what the Lord thy God has commanded thee, that do thou: add nothing to it; diminish nothing from it. Now unless that ye are able to prove that God has commanded your ceremonies, this his former commandment will damn both you and them.'

The preaching of Rough and Knox bore such fruit in St Andrews at that time that they decided to hold a Communion service in which not only the garrison but also some of the townspeople joined. It is probable that the two worked on their own form of service for this on the basis of the New Testament. It must have been shortly after this that John Rough left the castle, hoping to return, but the re-imposition of the siege prevented him and this left Knox in charge of the religious life of the garrison. From the time of his call he had warned the Castilians repeatedly that unless they repented they would come under the severe judgement of God, who would certainly allow them to be overcome and taken captive to France.

It appears that Knox did not have the same confidence as others had in the prospect of help from England. He may well have come to the conclusion that the French would act before the English, with disastrous results for the occupants of the castle. His prediction was fulfilled when on 29 June 1547, instead of the expected English army, the Castilians were dismayed to see a French fleet of twenty-one galleys under Leone Strozzi arrive. Their first action was to summon the Castilians to surrender. This they refused to do, still expecting English assistance. After an initial unsuccessful bombardment Strozzi landed soldiers who dragged canons near to the castle. A breach was made in the wall and the Castilians knew the game was up. They sent James Kirkcaldy of Grange to negotiate with the French commander and on 31 July the occupants surrendered.

Once the castle had capitulated, the French moved in and the prisoners, numbering some 120 men, were herded into the galleys. According to Knox, by the terms of surrender Strozzi had promised that they would be transported to France and once there they would be free to join the French king's army, or travel to any country of their choice, except Scotland. They were disillusioned when the fleet arrived in Rouen. The promises were not kept and, at the request of the pope and the governor Arran, the prisoners were condemned to perpetual captivity, the gentry in various castles in northern France, and those of the lowest orders as galley slaves aboard the French fleet.

Among the lowest orders was John Knox. He and the three Balfour brothers were condemned to the galleys as common criminals to spend the rest of their lives tugging at oars for the French monarch. They all worked in the same galley, the *Notre Dame*. The average galley was one hundred and fifty feet long with a beam of fifty feet. Usually propelled by twenty-five oars to a side, the galley would carry about 300 slaves who worked six to an oar, each chained to his bench. Down the centre of the galley ran a raised walk where the overseer could urge on by words and blows those lagging in the rowing. The galley slave's shelter was his bench and his food the barest rations above starvation. There was no question of privacy or sanitation. It was hard, unremitting and physically exhausting work.

The mental and spiritual conditions were equally hard to bear. The custom was to send felons to the galleys, and Knox and his companions found themselves mixing with some of the worst criminals of France. Knox could speak later of 'the torment I sustained in the galleys, which brought forth the sobs of my heart'. Attempts to convert the Scottish prisoners to Roman Catholicism were persistent and crude. They were paraded in chains to hear Mass and threatened with flogging and torture if they did not bow down to the Mass. 'But', said Knox, 'they could never make the poorest of the company to give reverence to that idol.' Knox seems to have exercised a leadership of the Scots galley slaves. On one occasion the captain of the *Notre Dame* and his lieutenant amused themselves by urging the Scots to kiss a painted image of the Virgin Mary. Knox steadfastly refused whereupon the officers forced the image into the hands of the objector who 'advisedly looking about' threw it overboard saying, 'Let "our Lady" now save herself; she is light enough; let her learn to swim.' After that episode the officers made no further attempts to have the Scots participate in such idolatry.

The *Notre Dame* formed part of a flotilla that sailed twice to Scotland in 1548. On the second occasion Knox was so desperately sick that those around him feared for his life. But Knox himself was confident that he would survive. At one point the galley was lying off St Andrews, with the town just visible. His fellow prisoner, James Balfour, raised him up and asked if he knew the place. 'Yes,' he answered, 'I know it well, for I see the steeple of that place where God first in public opened my mouth to his glory; and I am fully persuaded, how weak that ever I now appear, that I shall not depart this life till my tongue shall glorify his name in the same place.'

Attempts to convert the Castilians to Romanism were not confined to the galleys. The French ecclesiastical authorities sought to convert the gentry who were in the various prisons. In particular, they laboured assiduously to convert Henry Balnaves of Halhill who was imprisoned in the Old Palace in Rouen. This was without success for, according to Knox, he won all the debates which he had with the Romanist advocates. It may have been to strengthen himself against the Romanist arguments, or to clarify his own thinking, that Balnaves wrote a treatise on the doctrine of justification by faith.

Balnaves arranged for the manuscript of his treatise to be sent to Knox for his perusal and editing. At this time Knox says he was 'lying in irons and sore troubled by corporal infirmity', in the galley *Notre Dame*. Nevertheless he must have read the text with enthusiasm and set about editing it. He divided it into chapters and added some marginal notes. He also wrote a prefatory letter to his fellow prisoners, 'the best beloved brethren of the congregation of the Castle of St Andrews', encouraging them that however desperate their circumstances might seem, the godly would triumph in the end. It finished with the prayer: 'Hear, O Lord, and grant that as now with pen and ink, so shortly we may confess with voice and tongue the same before thy congregation.'

In his letter to the Castilians, Knox says that he revised and annotated Balnaves' treatise not merely to 'illustrate' it but 'to give my Confession of the article of justification therein contained'. Knox pointed out in 1566, when writing the first book of his *History*, that this treatise contained 'the sum of his doctrine and the confession of his faith'. 'The substance of justification is to cleave fast unto God by Jesus Christ.' All other methods of justification are of the devil whose plan God frustrates by bringing out a faithful seed who, believing, do not seek their own justification by the law. It was this desire for self-justification by the law that had led to the invention of man-made methods of salvation in the Church of Rome. Those who are justified are always required to bring forth good works as fruits of justification and as a proof of their faith.

Although Knox sent the treatise to Scotland for publication it is probable that it was too 'hot' an item to publish in 1548 and it may have circulated in manuscript among the Protestants. It disappeared, only to be found later in the papers of Lady Alison Sandilands, widow of Cockburn of Ormiston, by Knox's secretary, Richard Bannatyne, who first published it in 1584.

This statement is the first manifesto, the preliminary blast of the trumpet blown by Knox as the 'Trumpeter of God'. Although containing the Lutheran teaching, much of it more closely resembles the views expressed by John Calvin in his *Institutes of the Christian Religion*. During his time in the galleys Knox — although his physical frame was weakened — grew spiritually stronger. He emerged as the leader of the group, and maintained an equally forthright testimony as a prisoner of the French. He had come to hate and fear Roman Catholicism not only because he had suffered under the slave driver's lash for his Protestant beliefs but because he believed it destroyed men's souls by its idolatry. He was out to destroy it as the children of Israel were to bring down Jericho when they blew the trumpets around the walls of the city.

4

IN ENGLAND:

'that great rest'

The day came when Knox was released from the galleys. We are not told how or why he gained his freedom. It is conjectured that some of his friends made representations to the French king claiming that Knox had not been guilty of participation in Cardinal Beaton's murder. The release took place probably in March 1549.

On being released Knox had to decide where to go. If he followed his heart and returned to Scotland it would inevitably mean arrest, trial and death. England at that time was a safer place for friends of the reforming movement. Archbishop Cranmer was seeking to gather together a body of international Reformers who, under his leadership, would help with the work of remaking the Church of England, so Knox travelled to London where he received a warm welcome from the Protestant community. For the next five years he was to play an important part in the reforming work in England. He describes his time there as 'that great rest'.

Henry VIII had died on 28 January 1547, and was succeeded by his young son, Edward VI. He was a friend of the Protestant cause and so were the Lord Protector, the Duke of Somerset; and the Archbishop of Canterbury, Thomas Cranmer. The work to take the Reformation a stage further was hampered by an acute shortage of preachers. Soon after Knox's arrival, the Privy Council set about identifying qualified preachers and drew up a list of eighty suitable men. Knox was one of them and he was appointed to the border town of Berwick-upon-Tweed and to the parish church of St Mary's.

This fortified and overcrowded town presented a great challenge. A contemporary report said, 'The place is one of social disorder' and 'It will require a stern disciplinarian in the pulpit as well as a stirring preacher to work out a moral and social reform.' Increasing numbers flocked to hear Knox, including many Scots. Through his preaching, more and more people became acquainted with the new doctrines. Years later, in one of his rare boasts, he said to Mary, Queen of Scots, when accused of trouble-making:

> I shame not, Madam, further to affirm that God so blessed my weak labours that in Berwick (where commonly before there used to be slaughter by reason of quarrels among the soldiers) there was a quietness all the time that I remained as there is this day in Edinburgh.

At Berwick he came into friendship with the Bowes family. Richard Bowes was the captain of the nearby Norham Castle. His wife, Elizabeth, attended Knox's preaching in the parish church and identified with the reforming cause. She was prone to spiritual depression and often doubted whether a work of grace had taken place in her life. A correspondence began between her and Knox over her spiritual concerns, as he sought gently to counsel and encourage her. The letters between them that have been preserved reveal in Knox a tender and caring heart, and great skill in dealing with a Christian's inner conflicts. Knox fell in love with her daughter Marjory, who later became his wife.

In the early summer of 1551 Knox moved to Newcastle and to the Church of St Nicholas. His reputation was growing fast. He acquired a powerful new patron, John Dudley, Earl of Warwick, now Duke of Northumberland. The Duke took Knox as his chaplain and this meant an introduction to the Court of King Edward VI. Although he had the opportunity to preach in the Chapel Royal at Windsor there is some doubt about whether he was appointed one of the special chaplains to the king. In one sermon Knox launched with characteristic vigour into a lively attack on the practice of kneeling at the Communion. His objection to kneeling in receiving the elements led the Privy Council to insert in Cranmer's *Second Book of Common Prayer* a highly Protestant explanation of kneeling:

> *It is hereby declared, That thereby no adoration is intended, or ought to be done, either unto the Sacramental Bread or Wine there bodily received, or unto any Corporal Presence of Christ's natural Flesh and Blood.*

It was called 'the Black Rubric' because it was printed in black. 'A runagate Scot', records Dean Weston, 'did take away the adoring or worshipping of Christ in the sacrament, by whose procurement that heresy was put into the last *Common Book*. So much prevailed that one man's authority at that time.'

Knox had indeed become a formidable force in the progress of the Reformation in England and the Duke of Northumberland wrote to Sir William Cecil, Secretary of State, recommending his name for the vacant bishopric at Rochester. When offered this, Knox firmly refused, believing his true vocation was preaching, but also due to 'foresight of trouble to come'. In February 1553 he received a message telling him that he was to be appointed vicar of All-Hallows in Bread Street, London. He had no intention of accepting it. After preaching a controversial sermon on John 13:15 before the King at Whitehall Palace, concerning the treachery of counsellors, he was summoned before the Privy Council on 14 April 1553. Knox was questioned on why he refused the vicarage of All-Hallows and the bishopric of Rochester. Then they demanded to know why he did not kneel at Communion. In the end they told him they were sorry to see that he had a mind contrary to the common order, to which he replied that he was more sorry that the common order should be contrary to Christ's institution. Soon afterwards, he received word that he was to preach in Kent and then in Buckinghamshire, where he found a congenial congregation at Amersham.

It was while Knox was in Amersham that Edward VI died on 6 July 1553, at the age of sixteen. Before he died Edward, knowing that his sister Mary's sympathies were entirely Roman Catholic, took measures to safeguard the Protestant succession. Following discussions with the Duke of Northumberland it was agreed that he would bequeath his throne to Lady Jane Grey, the daughter of his Protestant cousin, the Duchess of Suffolk. The plan failed and on 19 July the Lord Mayor of London proclaimed Mary as Queen.

Knox, preaching to the large number of Protestants in Buckinghamshire, continued to denounce the Mass but found the situation worsening. In November 1553 Parliament repealed the laws that had been made in favour of church reform and restored Roman Catholicism to its former position as the religion of the realm. A month's grace was given to Protestants, but after that they would cease to have the protection of the law and could be arrested, tried and punished as heretics. 'That great rest', as Knox called it, was well and truly over.

Some of the leading Protestants fled to the Continent, including Edmund Grindal, Thomas Lever, John Foxe and Miles Coverdale. John à Lasco (a.k.a. Jan Laski) sailed from Gravesend with 175 of his congregation. Others were to remain and meet their deaths at the hand of Mary, including Thomas Cranmer, Hugh Latimer, Nicholas Ridley and John Hooper. Knox saw that things were becoming dangerous for him and returned to Newcastle. When it became apparent that to remain in England would mean death, he followed the counsel of friends and set sail for France, landing at Dieppe on 20 January 1554.

Knox knew that there was a colony of Scottish merchants in the thriving port of Dieppe and that he would be safe with them. While there he began to reflect and question his own motives for leaving England. He was tormented by conscience over his flight. The fear of death was not the chief cause, as he writes to Mrs Bowes:

And albeit that I have in the beginning of this battle appeared to play the faint-hearted and feeble soldier (the cause I remit to God) yet my prayer is I be restored to the battle again.

At that time Knox sent a pastoral letter to 'The Faithful in London, Newcastle and Berwick' — his three congregations. It is dated the last day of February 1554, 'from a sore troubled heart upon my departure from Dieppe, whither God knoweth'. Knox wanted to go to Switzerland to consult the Reformers there on the perilous situation confronting the church in both England and Scotland. His journey took him first to John Calvin at Geneva, and Calvin sent him on to Heinrich Bullinger, that 'Father of the Faith' in Zurich. Among the questions to which Knox was seeking an answer was 'Whether obedience is to be rendered to a magistrate who enforces idolatry and condemns true religion?' Bullinger's answers counselled patience and endurance in the struggle. Although he strongly held to the view that tyrants ought not to be obeyed, he was hesitant to endorse the idea of killing them. What Knox learned from his consultations, especially with Bullinger, helped shape his future thinking on this matter.

Having completed the consultations in Switzerland Knox hurried back to Dieppe at the beginning of May. From there he wrote *Two Comfortable Epistles to the Afflicted Brethren in England* on 10 and 31 May. They were exhortations to constancy. He stayed on in Dieppe for several months, but word received from across the water was not good. In England Mary Tudor had pressed through her Marriage Bill and Philip of Spain was preparing to sail from Corunna with an escort of 150 ships to marry her that summer at Westminster. Mary of Guise had taken on herself the sole Regency of Scotland. It was against this darkening background that on 20 July Knox published *A Faithful Admonition to the Professors of God's Truth in England*. It was partly a sermon based on Christ walking on the water, but he then went on to state what he believed to be the basic reason for the present evil situation. He blamed the preachers like himself and the political leaders. He then turned his attention to Queen Mary who had handed over England to the pope and to Philip of Spain, and said that 'under an English name she beareth a Spaniard's heart'. His regret that Mary had not been executed for idolatry was virtually a call to rebellion.

Concluding that he could do nothing more for England at that time, Knox set out once again for Geneva. His plan was to spend time studying Greek and Hebrew, and to read Calvin's theological writings as well as listen to him preach. At this time the Marian government was putting into operation the machinery that would eventually light the fires of Oxford, Gloucester and Smithfield. Many were to suffer martyrdom. Those who fled to the Continent became known as the Marian exiles. Frankfurt-am-Maine was one of the cities where a number of exiles, including William Whittingham, settled in June 1554. They planned to set up a church that conformed to their views of the Reformation, but some wished to retain the English *Prayer Book*. The group led by Whittingham called John Knox to be their minister and although he was more interested in staying in Geneva, Calvin pressed him to accept the invitation.

Knox began ministering there in November 1554 but soon found himself plunged into controversy over the use of the *Second Book of Common Prayer*. Knox took his stand on the fact that he could not use the Anglican liturgy because there were more superstitious elements in it than kneeling at Communion. On the advice of Calvin another order of service was drawn up and it was agreed to give it a trial. However, the situation in Frankfurt changed when

Richard Cox and a fresh batch of exiles arrived. At the first service Cox and his followers insisted that they should follow the *Prayer Book,* but when this was refused by the elders they carried on anyway. Knox preached against the *Book* and attacked the whole Church of England as being only half reformed. This brought a violent reaction and a congregational meeting was convened to consider the whole matter. Cox and his followers demanded that the church must have 'an English face'. Knox's response was: 'God grant it to have the face of Christ's Church.' The conflict resulted in the expulsion of Knox from the congregation at Frankfurt at the end of March 1555.

Knox returned to Geneva and the four years he was to spend there (with a break of some months in Scotland) were the most formative in his life. He was able to devote himself to study and make contact with Calvin and the other Reformers. Many of his own ideas were developed and he was prepared for a position of leadership in the movement for Reformation. Knox was followed to Geneva by William Whittingham and some of the other radical Protestants from Frankfurt. When, through Calvin's good offices, Whittingham, Thomas Wood and Anthony Gilby obtained permission to set up an English church in Geneva, the congregation began in November 1555 with a membership of about fifty. The founders of the Genevan Church took up the liturgy rejected at Frankfurt and added to it a collection of fifty English versions of the Psalms in metre. This was published in 1556 as *The Form of Prayers and Administration of the Sacraments etc. used in the English Congregation at Geneva and approved by the famous and godly learned man John Calvin.*

From its inception on 1 November the congregation declared itself to be 'truly reformed'. As a number of historians have pointed out, it was indeed the first Puritan Church. It was this first English congregation in Geneva which gave distinct and united witness to the conviction that the ordering of the visible church was to be determined solely by the rule of Scripture. Christopher Goodman and Anthony Gilby were elected the acting ministers 'in the absence of John Knox', whom they apparently still regarded as their minister by virtue of his call to Frankfurt. In England it was used by the Puritans; in Scotland it was to become the first service book of the Reformed Church in Scotland. Thus originated the English Church at Geneva, the cradle of Puritanism, and a paramount influence upon the Reformation in Scotland.

The 'troubles at Frankfurt' were a defining moment for Knox and for the English Reformation as a whole. The conflict at Frankfurt grew out of differences of principle. The real issue was whether tradition, even of only three or four years' life, should determine forms of worship and polity or whether the pattern should come from the New Testament. Knox came to the view that he could do nothing more to purge the English Church of 'the dregs of Popery'.

5

AT GENEVA:

'the most perfect school of Christ'

There were developments back home in Scotland that constrained Knox to leave Geneva for a time in 1555. In a letter Mrs Bowes begged him to come and rescue Marjory and herself from Mary Tudor's England. He set off and reached Berwick in the late summer of 1555, where he found a welcome. He then got encouraging news from Scotland: more and more people seemed to be turning against the Church of Rome. The Protestants felt that they needed a leader and Knox was the obvious choice. He slipped over the Border from Berwick and went secretly to Edinburgh in late September 1555. He probably stayed in the home of a well-known Protestant merchant, James Syme, where he met with active supporters of Protestantism.

He discovered that there was a far greater commitment to Protestantism than he had expected. Writing to Mrs Bowes on 4 November 1555, he acknowledges that the journey to Edinburgh was contrary to his own judgement:

> *yet I praise God for them who were the cause external of*
> *my resort to these quarters... If I had not seen it with my*
> *eyes, in my own country, I could not have believed it! Yea,*
> *mother, their fervency doth so ravish me, that I cannot but*
> *accuse and condemn my slothful coldness. God grant them*
> *their heart's desire.*

There was an overwhelming hunger for a new way. Matters were discussed with the Protestant lairds, among them John Erskine of Dun, one of the leaders. Knox toured different parts of the country preaching and meeting Protestant sympathizers. He spent much of the time at the home of Lord Sandilands of Calder House, Midcalder.

Knox tells how when it was reported to the Queen Regent that he had preached in Ayr, 'some were of divers opinions, some affirming that it was an Englishman'. A bishop said, 'Nay, no Englishman, but it is Knox, that knave'. His activities came to the attention of the church authorities. The Black Friars rashly summoned him to appear on a charge of heresy before a special commission led by John Hamilton, the Archbishop of St Andrews, on 15 May 1556, in Black Friars Church in Edinburgh. Perhaps they did not think he would come, but he did, with Erskine of Dun and others. When the Queen Regent, Mary of Guise, heard that Knox was to attend, she realized the trial would be the signal for public riots, and the summons was withdrawn on a technicality. Knox saw no reason to hurry away, preaching there twice a day with reckless boldness to 'a greater audience than ever before he had done in that town'. Writing to Mrs Bowes he says, 'The trumpet blew the old sound three days together till private houses of different largeness could not contain the voice of it... Rejoice, mother, the time of our deliverance approacheth'.

The leaders were so impressed with Knox and the possibility of a new church that they persuaded him to write a letter to the Queen Regent pleading for the people of Scotland a settlement for the new Kirk. Glencairn delivered the letter to the Regent and they waited in vain for an answer. Knox heard afterwards that having glanced through it she handed it over to the Archbishop of Glasgow with the remark: 'Please you my Lord to read a pasquil [a practical joke].' She was not going to change. Knox was hurt and disappointed.

After this, Knox decided to head back to Geneva, arriving there on 13 September 1556. The English congregation there wanted him to minister to them. However, his departure did not placate the anger of the ecclesiastical authorities in Scotland. Immediately after he left, the bishops met once again, condemned him and burned him in effigy, an action which caused him to write his 'Appellation' in which he called upon the nobles for total reform of the church. Before leaving he made it quite clear that he would be prepared to return to Scotland when there were more Protestants and the nobles had called for him. In the meantime in a 'Letter of Wholesome Counsel' which he published later, he advised them how to organize their 'Privy Kirks'.

It was concluded that the brethren in every town at certain times should assemble together to Common Prayers, to exercise and reading of the Scriptures, till it should please God to give the sermon of exhortation to some for comfort and instruction of the rest.

Then, 'there should be confession of sins, invocation of the Spirit of the Lord Jesus, reading of passages from the Old and New Testaments, followed by exposition, thanksgiving and intercession.' These were the first directions given for the introduction of Reformed worship in Scotland. John Leslie, a Catholic writer, later observed how the Protestant preaching went on 'in chimney nooks, secret holes and such private places to trouble the whole country.'

Back in Geneva in May 1557 Knox received visitors from Scotland. They were James Syme, his host during his last stay in Edinburgh, and James Barron, one of the leading merchants of the city. They arrived with a letter signed by four of the Protestant noblemen. It declared that the believers whom Knox knew in Scotland were standing firm and had 'ane [one] godly thirst and desire, day by day', for his presence among them. The noblemen wrote:

> *If the Spirit of God will so move and permit time unto you, we will heartily desire you, in the name of the Lord, that ye will return again to these parts, where ye shall find all faithful that ye left behind, not only glad to hear your doctrine, but will be ready to jeopard lives and goods in the forward-setting of the glory of God.*

The call from Scotland was not unwelcome. When Knox sought the advice of Calvin and his other colleagues in Geneva they told him they believed that he should obey the summons.

In September 1557 Knox set off for Scotland once again and after a hazardous journey came to Dieppe on 23 October. On his arrival he found letters awaiting him which stated that as the Scottish nobles felt the time was not ripe he had better postpone his visit. The enthusiasm of those who had been most anxious for him to return had waned. The nobles were apparently trying to work out some kind of compromise with the Queen Regent since they did not feel that they could legitimately or effectively bring about a religious revolution by the use of force. For Knox no compromise was possible with a Regent who was determined to maintain both French and Roman Catholic power intact. On 27 October he dispatched a letter to the nobles in the hope that they would change their minds and renew the invitation. The text of the letter is in Knox's *History of the Reformation in Scotland.*

Letters he received in reply forced him to clarify his own thinking on the subject of rebellion for righteousness' sake. News came to him of the continuing persecution in England under Mary Tudor; Ridley, Latimer, Cranmer and Hooper had all perished in the flames. The church was being decimated. Persecution of Protestants in France was on the increase, and in Scotland and England he saw the malevolent operations of female monarchs. The cruel persecution of Mary in England goaded him to action. Because woman had usurped the natural authority of man she was causing most of the problems now faced by the true believers. The subject of women bearing rule was one on which Knox had thought long and hard, and on which he had done a great deal of reading. In his frustration he decided to write on the subject and on how it should be ended. He spent the latter part of his stay in Dieppe drawing up the work which he called *The First Blast of the Trumpet against the Monstrous Regiment of Women.* It was directed against what Knox regarded as the unnatural reign of women. After completing this work and having received no further encouragement from Scotland, Knox decided to return to Geneva through the centre of France, encouraging Protestant groups in different places.

Back in Geneva in the Spring of 1558 he settled down once again to his pastoral duties, preaching, writing and publishing. It was during this period that he worked out his theory of 'a godly revolution' which was to bear much fruit over the centuries. The book he had written while in Dieppe was published anonymously without author, publisher or place. It was for a time attributed to Christopher Goodman who had written and published on 1 January 1558 a work entitled *How Superior Powers Ought to be Obeyed of their Subjects*. The real point of the writing was how subjects ought to disobey non-Christian or popish rulers. It was only after some months that Knox revealed his identity as the author of *The First Blast*. In it he declared:

To promote a woman to bear rule, superiority, dominion or empire, above any realm, nation or city is repugnant to nature, contumely to God, a thing most contrarious to his revealed will and approved ordinance, and, finally, it is a subversion of all equity and justice.

In publishing this work he fully expected a storm and he was not disappointed. A year after its publication Knox was forced to admit: 'My *First Blast* has blown from me all my friends in England.' Many who supported Elizabeth when she came to the English throne later that year raised an outcry against the book. Elizabeth herself deeply resented the book and never forgave Knox for writing it.

As well as pastoring the English congregation in Geneva, Knox wrote several pamphlets. He was also involved in the production of a new translation of the Bible that was being prepared under the direction of his colleague in the ministry, William Whittingham. The Bible was completed in 1560 and became known as the Geneva Bible. This Bible, with its marginal notes, was to have a tremendous impact on the English and Scottish Reformations. It became very popular and went through more than one hundred and thirty editions, the last in 1644. It was used by the Reformers and Puritans, by the Pilgrim Fathers, by Shakespeare and by Oliver Cromwell. The Geneva Bible was the first English Bible to be published in Scotland and remained the preferred translation there long after the King James, or Authorized, Version came into use.

When Knox first reached Geneva, Calvin was moulding the church to what he believed was the biblical pattern. It was for the future good of the Reformed Church in Scotland that Knox was there at such a critical time. In a letter to a friend he declares:

> In my heart I would have wished, yea and cannot cease to wish, that it would please God to guide and conduct yourself to this place, where I neither fear nor shame to say is the most perfect school of Christ that ever was on the earth since the days of the apostles. In other places I confess Christ to be truly preached; but manners and religion so sincerely reformed I have not yet seen in any other place.

6

BACK TO SCOTLAND:

'John Knox is come'

Meanwhile in Scotland things were changing for the better. Knox's letters had reached their destination and on 3 December 1557, the Lords of the Congregation met in Edinburgh to consider what they ought to do. After careful deliberation they drew up and signed a *Godlie Band for maintenance of the Evangell* in which they said,

> *We, perceiving how Satan in his members, the Anti-christs of our time, cruelly doth rage, seeking to overthrow and to destroy the Evangel of Christ and His Congregation, ought, according to our bounden duty, to strive in our Master's cause, even unto the death, being certain of the victory in Him; the which our duty, being well considered, we do promise before the majesty of God and His Congregation: That we, by His grace, shall with all diligence continually apply our whole power, substance, and our very lives, to maintain, set forward, and establish the most blessed Word of God and His Congregation, and shall labour at our possibility to have faithful ministers, purely and truly*

*to minister Christ's Evangel and Sacraments to His people.
We shall maintain them, nourish them, and defend them,
the whole Congregation of Christ, and every member
thereof, at our whole powers and waring of our lives against
Satan and all wicked power that does intend tyranny or
trouble against the foresaid Congregation. Unto the which
holy Word and Congregation, we do join us, and also do
forsake and renounce the Congregation of Satan with all
the superstitions, abominations, and idolatry thereof.
And, moreover, shall declare ourselves manifestly enemies
thereto, by this our faithful promise before God, testified to
his Congregation by our subscriptions at these presents. At
Edinburgh, the third day of December, the year of God 1557
years. God called to witness.*

The signatories comprised the fourth Earl of Argyll and
his son Lord Lorne, the Earls of Glencairn and Morton, and
John Erskine of Dun. This was followed by a programme
for Reformed worship proposed by the 'lords and barons
professing Jesus Christ', which provided for the reading of
Edward VI's *Book of Common Prayer* weekly in every parish
church and for Protestant preaching in private. They also
agreed that the Reformed teachers should teach in private
houses only, until the government allowed them to do so in
public. This agreement led some of the preachers to become
private chaplains to the nobles and to exercise their ministries
within the safety of the homes of the nobles. Having made
these resolutions they then renewed their invitation to Knox
to return, writing at the same time to Calvin to ask him to
use his influence to encourage Knox to accept. Because of the
difficulties of finding a reliable messenger, however, almost a
year was to elapse before these letters arrived in Geneva.

In Scotland the hopes of the Congregation for some redress from the Queen Regent were dashed by the condemnation and burning of the eighty-two-year-old preacher, Walter Mill (or Mylne) (c. 1476–1558), on 28 April 1558. He was convicted of heresy and adjudged worthy of death but so great was the sympathy felt for the heroic old saint that no magistrate could be found who was willing to pronounce sentence, until a disreputable minion of the archbishop did so. As the martyr was being led to the stake, his great age and tottering steps deeply stirred the multitude of onlookers. Overcoming all weakness and pain, he declared from the flames: 'I am fourscore and two years old, and could not live long by the course of nature; but a hundred better shall arise out of the ashes of my bones.' 'Which thing', as Knox explains, 'did so highly offend the hearts of all godly, that immediately after his death began a new fervency among the people.' It could be said that Mill's burning rang the death knell of the papacy in Scotland. It did not, as hoped, terrorize the populace; it merely caused a flurry of oaths and covenants being sworn to defend the persecuted with force of arms.

The Congregation, realizing that 'faggot, fire and sword' was all they would get from the Queen Regent, presented a petition seeking reform of the church and state. They appealed for the common prayers to be read in their own language, for the Scriptures to be interpreted by godly and learned persons, for baptism and the Lord's Supper (in both kinds) to be ministered (again, in their own language), and for reform of the clergy. When Mary of Guise suppressed their letter to Parliament attacking the hierarchy, the Congregation presented a 'protestation' to Parliament in December 1558 in favour of 'the reformation of abuses in religion only'.

In England on 17 November 1558, Mary Tudor died, to be succeeded by her half-sister Elizabeth. Elizabeth was a nominal Protestant because of the Roman Catholic denial of her legitimacy, and her succession was a source of great joy to the Marian exiles. They were anxious to go back to England, and on 14 January 1559, the city council of Geneva granted them permission to depart and wished them well. The change placed Knox in an uncertain position. Without a congregation to which to minister, there was no valid reason for remaining in Geneva. Where would he go? He had not endeared himself to Englishmen and particularly to the bishops. These considerations, together with Elizabeth's antipathy to *The First Blast,* ensured that in God's providence Scotland seemed the only place to go.

He set off for home and on 19 February 1559 arrived at Dieppe. He sent a letter to Sir William Cecil requesting a safe conduct through England. While waiting for a reply he turned his attention to the Protestant church of Dieppe, where ministers had been placed through Calvin and the Genevan consistory. The congregation had experienced difficulties and Knox threw himself into the work. Through his ministry a number of the local gentry and ladies, including some royal officials, became Protestants. It was later that year in May that the first French Reformed Synod was held in Paris. Knox would have seen the proposed Confession of Faith and form of discipline. After sending a third letter to Scotland and receiving no response Knox decided to set sail on 22 April 1559 in a ship going to Leith, the port of Edinburgh. He duly arrived there on 2 May. His arrival was the signal for the release of pent-up forces: 'John Knox is come.'

7

CONTENDING:

'I see the battle shall be great'

In Scotland the new fervency following the cruel death of Walter Mill resulted in increasing militancy on the part of the Protestants in Dundee, Perth and some of the east-coast burghs (boroughs). In March 1559, two months prior to the return of Knox, a proclamation had been made at the market cross in Edinburgh by order of the Queen Regent that no person was to preach or administer the sacraments without authority from the bishops. The proclamation was ignored by four of the Reformed preachers, Paul Methven, John Christison, William Harlaw and John Willock. The Queen Regent then charged the four ministers with usurping the ministerial office and preaching sedition. They were summoned to stand trial before the Court of Justiciary in Stirling on 10 May 1559. Messages were sent to the Queen Regent begging her not to interfere with the preachers unless they were teaching false doctrine, but she had replied that they would be banished from Scotland 'even if they preached as truly as ever did St Paul'.

The state of Knox's mind when he received this news can be gauged from the following letter to Mrs Anne Locke, written in haste on the day after his arrival:

These few lines are to signify unto you, dear sister, that it has pleased the merciful providence of my heavenly Father to conduct me to Edinburgh, where I arrived the 2nd of May: uncertain as yet what God shall further work in this country, except I see the battle shall be great, for Satan rageth even to the uttermost; and I am come, I praise my God, even in the brunt of the battle. For my fellow preachers have a day appointed to answer before the Queen Regent, the 10th of this instant, when I intend (if God impede not) also to be present; be life, be death, or else by both, to glorify his godly name, who thus mercifully has heard my long cries. Assist me, sister, with your prayers, that now I shrink not, when the battle approaches.

The next day he set off for Dundee where he found the Protestants in Angus and Mearns already assembled. They were determined to accompany their ministers to the place of trial and to avow their own adherence to the doctrines for which the ministers were accused. The providential arrival of such a leader at this point must have been encouraging to the assembly. The liberty of Knox accompanying them to Stirling was readily granted. Lest the unexpected approach of such a multitude should alarm or offend the Queen Regent, they agreed to stop at Perth and sent John Erskine, the Laird of Dun, to Stirling to assure the Queen Regent that they were unarmed and were appearing simply in support of their ministers. The Queen again resorted to deceit. She persuaded Erskine to ask his brethren to desist from the journey, authorizing him to promise in her name that she would put a stop to the trial. The majority trusted in the royal promise and returned to their homes. But the Queen Regent's double dealing soon came to light. She and her council suddenly summoned the preachers again to come on 10 May and, without giving them time to get there, were outlawed for non-appearance, and all were prohibited, under the pain of rebellion, from harbouring or assisting them.

Meanwhile Knox remained in Perth. 'Now he became', as Sir James Croft reported to Sir William Cecil a little later, 'the centre of the Reformation movement.' St John's Kirk in the centre of the town occupied such a prominent place in the community that the burgh was generally known as 'St Johnstoun.' Knox preached a powerful sermon against broken faith, lies, deceit and the idolatry of the Mass and image worship. The sermon passed off without incident but shortly afterwards one of the local priests went into the church to celebrate Mass. As the priest prepared to take out the Host a young boy who had heard Knox preach shouted out in protest. The priest heard him, turned round and struck him a sharp blow. The boy picked up a stone and threw it at the priest. It missed him but struck one of the statues. The result was uproar. In a few moments the altar, images and ornaments had all been thrown down and trampled under foot. The noise attracted others who, in spite of the appeals of the magistrates and preachers, went on to attack the monasteries of the Black and Grey Friars and the magnificent Charterhouse of the Carthusian monks. They pushed their way past the guards and broke all the religious statues they could find. In his *History of the Reformation* Knox distanced himself from the events of that day, declaring that 'the rascal multitude' were responsible.

The Queen Regent then threatened retaliation, using a small army of eight or nine hundred French soldiers. The Protestants were doing all in their power to put the burgh in a state of defence. They had drawn up an army of three thousand on the large open space known as the Inch. Realizing that she was outnumbered, the Queen Regent decided to negotiate. The Protestant leaders told her that if she allowed the true religion to proceed in peace there would be no trouble. They did not intend rebellion but merely the protection of their unjustly persecuted brethren. On 28 May, an agreement was reached that both armies would disband leaving the Queen Regent to enter Perth but none of the inhabitants were to be punished for the recent troubles.

However, on entering Perth, the Queen Regent persecuted some of the leading Protestants there, and on quitting it some days later she left an occupying garrison of Scottish mercenaries in the pay of the French. Lord James Stewart (later Regent) and the Earl of Argyll, who had until then sided with her, had had enough of her broken promises and now committed themselves to the cause of the Congregation. On 31 May they and the other Lords entered into a solemn bond 'faithfully promising to assist and defend one another against all persons that would pursue for religion's sake'. They resolved 'to effect reformation in all the places where they had authority and where the majority of the people were in favour of it — abolishing Catholicism and establishing Protestant worship'.

True to their purpose, the Lords decided to press forward to further the Reformation in St Andrews where Knox arranged to rendezvous with them. He rode first to Crail on the south coast of Fife, where, on 9 June, he preached a stirring sermon, denouncing the Queen Regent for violating the truce. The local people destroyed all the altars and images in the church. The next day he preached in Anstruther to similar effect. In the light of this, Archbishop Hamilton hurried to St Andrews with an armed force, swearing that if Knox tried to preach there he would be shot on sight: 'He should make him be saluted with a dozen of culverings (muskets), whereof the most part should light upon his nose.' This threat from the Archbishop, together with the presence of the Queen Regent and her French troops only twelve miles away at Falkland, led Knox's supporters to counsel him against preaching in St Andrews. The valiant Reformer, however, remained undeterred and replied to his advisers:

> I beseech your honours not to stop me to present myself unto my brethren. As for the fear of danger that may come to me, let no man be solicitous; for my life is in the custody of him whose glory I seek; and therefore I cannot so fear their boast nor tyranny, that I will cease from doing my duty when God of his mercy offereth the occasion. I desire the hand nor weapon of no man to defend me. I only crave audience, which if it be denied here unto me at this time, I must seek further where I may have it.

On Sunday 11 June Knox entered the pulpit of the parish church in St Andrews and preached before a numerous congregation (which included many scholars from the university) without any interruption. His subject was Christ's cleansing of the temple in Jerusalem, ejecting the buyers and sellers, and overthrowing the tables of the money changers. Knox took the opportunity to expose and denounce the various corruptions which the papacy had introduced and to point out the way of reform. He preached on four successive days with such effect that the Provost and citizens of St Andrews agreed to set up Reformed worship in the town, and a number of priests confessed faith in the Lord Jesus Christ — 'for no less than twenty one "maisters" [priests] made renunciation of the old faith and profession of the new'.

For Knox the experience of preaching once more in St Andrews was rewarding. On 23 June he wrote to Anne Locke: 'The long thirst of my wretched heart is satisfied in abundance', and added that for the past forty days and more 'God used my tongue in my native country to the manifestation of his glory'. The Word of God began to triumph in the hearts and lives of many hearers, and the Reformed cause made swift progress in the land. In a letter written on 2 September 1559, Knox said,

> *I have been in continual travel and notwithstanding the fevers that have vexed me the space of a month, yet have I travelled through the most part of this realm where, all praise be to his blessed Majesty, men of all sorts and conditions embrace the truth. We do nothing but go about Jericho, blowing with trumpets as God giveth strength, hoping victory by his power alone.*

Knox had written to Calvin about several matters, including the administration of baptism in certain cases. In his reply Calvin stated: 'We are astonished at such incredible progress in so brief a space of time, so we likewise give thanks to God whose singular blessing is signally displayed herein.'

8

CIVIL WAR:

'blowing the Master's trumpet'

The Queen Regent wanted to subject Scotland politically to the authority of France. The plan was that if she was to die without leaving an heir, the King of France was to become King of Scotland. There was a growing French presence in Scotland. Frenchmen held many of the chief posts in government and to reinforce the Regent's authority more and more French troops were entering the country. If she got her way the Church of Rome would be fully restored, and Protestantism would be crushed out of existence. The Lords of the Congregation were determined that Mary should not have her way, and in this they had the support of a growing number of Scottish people. The result was a civil war that lasted until July 1560.

After the confrontation at St Andrews, Mary retired to Edinburgh Castle, and Knox and the congregation went back to Perth. They then moved toward Stirling, which they captured. After that they marched towards Edinburgh. The Queen Regent, fearing she would be trapped, made for Dunbar Castle on the edge of the North Sea, where she would be safe until help arrived from France or she could make her escape by sea. On 30 June 1559, the army of the Congregation moved into Edinburgh. Knox went to the pulpit of St Giles and preached a sermon. The next day the Queen Regent issued letters declaring that the actions of the Congregation were intent on subverting her authority. She ordered them to leave Edinburgh within six hours. Ignoring her commands they stayed where they were, and on 7 July, they flocked into the Edinburgh Tolbooth to elect Knox as minister of St Giles. In spite of this, the Congregation knew that it was only a matter of time before a French fleet would come to assist the Queen Regent.

The Lords of the Congregation were aware that their best hope of help lay with the English. They decided to appoint Knox to negotiate with Sir William Cecil, Queen Elizabeth's Secretary of State. Any negotiation between the English court and the Scottish Protestants would have to be conducted with the utmost secrecy. Knox had to convince Cecil that they were concerned only with the establishment of the true religion and perpetual peace with England. The Congregation seized Scotland's coining irons from the mint at Holyrood House. The Protestants would produce coins themselves, without any reference to French sovereignty. In the light of this defiance of her authority Mary of Guise decided to march on Edinburgh. Her army seized and occupied Leith. The Congregation negotiated and an agreement was reached at Leith Links on 23 July 1559. The Congregation gave back the coining irons, handed over the Palace of Holyrood House and retired. The Queen Regent returned to Edinburgh and took up residence in the castle once more to await reinforcements from France.

Knox had been commissioned to negotiate mutually acceptable terms between the Scottish Protestants and Elizabeth I. If Elizabeth supplied them with men and money the Scottish Protestants were ready to make a firm league with England. At this juncture King Henri II of France died suddenly. The husband of the young Mary, Queen of Scots, became King of France, and Mary became Queen. Under the new monarchy the Queen Regent's brothers became highly influential at the French Court and it seemed increasingly likely that she would be sent help from France against the Reformers. Efforts were now made to oust Mary of Guise.

The Lords met in Stirling on 15 October 1559 and decided that the time had come to depose the Queen Regent. They marched into Edinburgh three days later only to find that she had slipped away to the safety of Leith, which was garrisoned by French soldiers. The Lords of the Congregation met on 21 October and suspended her commission as Regent. The country was now officially ruled by a Great Council of thirty leading Protestants.

However, things were not going well. A thousand pounds sent by the English was intercepted and seized by one of Mary of Guise's supporters. At the beginning of November Protestant morale abruptly collapsed and the Congregation decided to withdraw from Edinburgh and retreated to Linlithgow and then to Stirling.

Alarmed by the reports he was hearing, Knox, who had been preaching in St Giles, went with them to Stirling, seeking to sustain their courage. There in the Church of the Holy Rood, he preached one of the most influential sermons of his life. Arran, who had now finally aligned himself to the cause of the Congregation, was there along with other lords. Knox based his sermon on the very passage in Psalm 80 from which he had preached in Edinburgh on the previous Lord's Day. The Psalm speaks of God rooting out the heathen, and planting a great vine only to see it attacked by wild animals, burned by fire and cut down. He dismissed the idea that God was angry with them for having taken up the sword of self-defence. It was because of their sins that God was withholding his blessing and, after some very pointed application of this to his hearers, and calls to repentance, a note of strong encouragement was struck. God often permitted the wicked to triumph for a while, and exposed his chosen people to mockery, dangers and apparent destruction, in order to humble them and to reveal their own weakness, and make them look to him for deliverance and victory. If they turned in all sincerity to God they would be heard. Knox was in no doubt that their present distress would be followed by success. He concluded :

Yea, whatsoever shall become of us and of our mortal carcases, I doubt not but this cause, in despite of Satan, shall prevail in the realm of Scotland. For, as it is the eternal truth of the eternal God, so shall it once prevail, howsoever for a time it may be impugned!

The sermon had a powerful effect upon the hearers. Knox's words restored the confidence of the Lords of the Congregation and they held a meeting of the council with Knox called in to say the prayers. God was on their side and victory would be theirs. The sermon was a fine illustration of what Thomas Randolph, Queen Elizabeth's envoy to Scotland, said of Knox in one of his dispatches: 'I assure you, the voice of that one man is able in one hour to put more life into us, than five hundred trumpets continually blustering in our ears!' Knox blew his Master's trumpet with no uncertain sound, and his rallying calls were used by God to great effect.

For some time the nobles had been appealing for aid from England and at that meeting they authorized William Maitland of Lethington to go immediately to London to press their case. Knox himself was in frequent correspondence about the matter. On 18 November he addressed a letter to Sir William Cecil, to whom he pointed out that many of the Protestant Lords were so impoverished as a result of fighting the French forces that they could do no more. If therefore the French should gain control of Scotland, the conquest of England would be next on the agenda.

It took much effort to persuade Queen Elizabeth that it was in England's best interests to come to Scotland's aid. With French troops on its borders there was considerable unease in England, where it was common knowledge that the destruction of Scottish Protestantism was a prelude to dethroning Elizabeth in favour of Mary Stuart, Queen of Scotland and France. Knox wrote a very strong warning to Sir James Croft, Captain of Berwick Castle and Warden of the East Marches. In his letter Knox sought to broker a means for English support. Not wishing unduly to provoke the French, England cautiously and very secretly first sent gold to help the Scots. In December 1559 the Duke of Norfolk was appointed Lord Lieutenant in the Northern Counties with instructions to prepare an army to go to the aid of the Scots and expel the French.

At last on 22 January a small fleet of English ships was sighted at the mouth of the Firth of Forth. Queen Elizabeth had finally sent help. Admiral Wilson had set sail from Gillingham on 27 December 1559, with fourteen vessels.

On the way up he had encountered dreadful storms and lost six vessels. The same storms struck the large French fleet on its way to relieve the French in Scotland and only 900 soldiers eventually arrived at Leith. At the end of January Queen Elizabeth sent the Duke of Norfolk to Berwick to negotiate with the Scottish Protestants. Arran, Lord James Stewart, Lord Ruthven and several other members of the Congregation travelled south to meet him.

On 27 February 1560, the Treaty of Berwick was signed. The English Queen understood that the French intended to conquer Scotland, suppress its liberties and unite it to the crown of France. Elizabeth would take into her protection the realm of Scotland in order to preserve them in their old freedoms and liberties and keep them from conquest. She would speedily send an army north to expel the French from Scotland. If England were invaded by the French the Scots would send an army to English aid. The treaty did not mention religious matters but the 'liberties' of the Scots.

On 29 March an English army marched north and joined Arran and his force at Prestonpans. Mary of Guise found refuge in Edinburgh Castle and a force of 11,000 English soldiers and 2,000 Scottish mercenaries began to besiege Leith which was defended by some 4,000 French troops.

In mid April Knox was able to enter Edinburgh once more. Another Covenant was sworn on 27 April 1560, declaring:

> we altogether in general, and every one of us in special, by himself, with our bodies, goods, friends, and all that we may do, shall set forward the Reformation of Religion, according to God's Word; and procure, by all means possible, that the truth of God's word have free passage within this realm.

The forty-nine signatories to the Covenant were the most powerful landholders in Scotland and the document itself promulgated two new and substantial doctrines: 1) that the people are the custodians of the Word of God; and 2) that the people of Scotland are the rightful conservators of their own ancient freedoms and liberties, among which is government by native sovereigns and magistrates, according to use.

It took three months for the siege to end, and when it did, it was not because the Leith defences had been breached; other things happened to hasten the peace. Mary of Guise was seriously ill and knew she was dying. She sent for her Lords and urged them to favour the alliance with France and turn away from England. With her death on 11 June 1560, the rising tide of Protestantism and the anti-French feeling now made possible the very alliance she had tried to prevent. On 16 June, commissioners from England and France met to conclude negotiations and on 6 July the Treaty of Edinburgh was signed. The principal clause said that all foreign troops were to withdraw from Scotland. Since the Scots 'had spontaneously and freely professed and acknowledged their obedience and loyalty to their said most Christian king and queen', Francois and Mary would fulfil all the obligations in the treaty. Everything relating to religion was to be referred to the Scottish Parliament.

The Treaty of Edinburgh was a glorious triumph for independence and for Protestantism. It marked the end of the 'auld alliance' between Scotland and France and the beginning of a new amicable relationship between the English and the Scots. On Sunday 19 July 1560, John Knox led a great public service of thanksgiving in St Giles for the success that had crowned their endeavours, remembering in his fervent prayers 'our confederates of England, the instruments by whom we are now set at liberty'.

> We beseech thee, therefore, O Father of mercies, that as of thy undeserved grace thou hast partly removed our darkness, suppressed idolatry and taken from above our heads the devouring sword of merciless strangers, that so it would please thee to proceed with us in this thy grace begun.

9

THE NEW BEGINNING:

'the face of Christ's Kirk'

Although the Treaty of Berwick did not mention church reform it actually cleared the way for it. The Three Estates, the Scottish Parliament, met on 1 August 1560. Taking advantage of a hitherto neglected privilege, many of the lesser landlords came to this Parliament, increasing its Protestant slant. The continued absence of a royal head, following the Regent's death, gave to the nation the aspect of a republic rather than a kingdom. Parliament boldly gave the people what they seemed to crave.

In the *History of the Reformation in Scotland*, Knox gives a record of the events. A supplication was laid before the Parliament by the Protestant nobility, decrying the corruptions of Roman Catholicism, and seeking the abolition of popery. The petition of the Protestants exclaimed:

We offer ourselves to prove, that in all the [rabble of the] clergy there is not one lawful minister, if God's Word, the practice of the apostles, and their own ancient laws shall

judge of lawful election. We further offer ourselves to prove
them all thieves and murderers: yea, rebels and traitors
to the lawful authority of empires, kings, and princes;
and therefore unworthy to be suffered in any reformed
commonwealth.

In response, the Parliament directed the Protestant noblemen and ministers to draw up 'in plain and several heads, the sum of that doctrine which they would maintain, and would desire this present Parliament to establish as wholesome, true, and only necessary to be believed and to be received within this realm'.

Over the next four days, the *Scots Confession* was drafted by six ministers, all with the same Christian name: John Winram, John Spottiswoode, John Willock, John Douglas, John Row and John Knox. On 17 August 1560, the document was read twice, article by article, before the Parliament; and the Protestant ministers stood ready to defend the cause of truth, in the event of any objection to an article of belief. When the vote was taken, the *Confession* was ratified, with only a few dissenting voices, who 'yet for their dissenting could produce no better reason but, "We will believe as our fathers believed".' Knox adds: 'The bishops (papistical, we mean), spake nothing.'

On 24 August 1560, the Parliament enacted that in all time coming the pope of Rome should have 'no jurisdiction nor authority within this realm', annulled all past legislation contrary to the *Confession*, and prohibited the saying or hearing of Mass, with pains and penalties of confiscation and imprisonment for all who refused to comply.

It was natural that Knox and his fellow Reformers should be eager to accept the opportunity to declare their faith publicly and so to defend themselves against the charge of heresy commonly brought against them by their enemies both at home and abroad. Since the Reformation claimed above all else to be a return to the pure gospel and scriptural truth, it was entirely appropriate that as the foundation of a Reformed Church there should be drawn up a Confession of Faith. The Confession embodies the spirit of the Scottish Reformers. It has been described by Peter Lorimer as 'the warm utterance of a people's heart'. It is a simple straightforward document stating in plain language their general creedal position and revealing conviction, determination and enthusiasm. The principal influence was undoubtedly from Geneva, for Calvin's *Catechism* and especially the Confession of the English congregation there clearly provided the foundation.

In the Preface the writers begin with a benediction reminiscent of the Pauline epistles:

> *The Estates of Scotland with the inhabitants of the same, professing Christ Jesus his holy Evangel, to their natural countrymen, and to all other realms and nations, professing the same Lord Jesus with them, wish grace, peace, and mercy from God the Father of our Lord Jesus Christ, with the spirit of righteous judgment, for salutation... Long have we thirsted, dear brethren, to have notified unto the world the sum of that doctrine which we profess and for the which we have sustained infamy and danger.*

Then there comes a declaration of openness:

> *... protesting that if any man will note in this our Confession any Article or sentence repugnant to God's Holy Word,*

that it would please him of his gentleness and for Christian charity's sake to admonish us of the same in writing; and we, of our honour and fidelity, do promise unto him satisfaction from the mouth of God, that is, from His Holy Scriptures, or else reformation of that which he shall prove to be amiss.

The *Confession* affirms the Reformed Faith with a simple fervour. The doctrine of eternal election out of mere grace is closely tied to that of the mediation of Christ. By grace we become the sons of God and are not afraid to call him our Father. Good works flow unfailingly from Christ's indwelling Spirit and stress is laid upon them 'to the profit of our neighbours'. There is a lively description of the one true church — catholic in that it contains the elect of all ages, realms and races, and invisible since 'God alone knows whom he has chosen.' It is not, however, so invisible as not to be discerned from the false church — 'the Kirk malignant', 'the pestilent synagogue which Satan has decked with the name of the Kirk'. The notes (or marks) of the true church are:

neither antiquity, title usurped, lineal descent, place appointed, nor multitude of men approving an error but are: 1) the true preaching of the Word of God; 2) the right administration of the Sacraments: and 3) ecclesiastical discipline, uprightly ministered, as God's Word prescribes, whereby vice is repressed and virtue nourished.

The section on the sacraments is careful to reject the view of those who affirm the sacraments 'to be nothing else but naked and bare signs' and also:

*any transubstantiation of bread into Christ's natural body
and of wine into his natural blood as the Papists have
perniciously taught and damnably believed; but this union
and communion which we have with the body and blood of
Christ Jesus in the right use of the sacraments, is wrought
by operation of the Holy Ghost, who by true faith carries
us above all things that are visible, carnal and earthly, and
makes us to feed upon the body and blood of Christ Jesus
which was once broken and shed for us, which is now in
heaven, and appears in the presence of his Father for us.*

A note of doxology is perhaps the distinctive note of the
Scots Confession, in which faith ever and again finds expression in worship. It is sounded for the last time at the close
of the final section; and then praise blends almost imperceptibly into prayer as the confessors recall in conclusion
the needs of their world, the imperative obligations of their
missionary task, and the inexhaustible riches of their God.

*Arise, O Lord, and let Thy enemies be confounded; let them
flee from Thy presence that hate Thy godly name. Give Thy
servants strength to speak Thy Word in boldness, and let all
nations cleave to Thy true knowledge. Amen.*

The next question that faced the Reformers was: What
form should the new church take? Should it be a church
purified by an adaptation of the old or should something
new be put in its place? On 29 April 1560, immediately
following the band or contract by the Lords of the
Congregation to 'set forward the Reformation of Religion',
the 'Great Council of the Realm' or Protestant provisional
government, commissioned 'a Book of Reformation'. It is

reckoned that Knox was responsible for the original idea of preparing the book and was probably largely responsible for its contents. He had been concerned to have a plan in hand for the new church's organization which would be implemented immediately when victory had been achieved. The work was completed in twenty days and submitted to the Lords of the Congregation on 20 May 1560. However, with the English and French armies facing each other, everything was moving to a military crisis. Consequently no action was taken except that the book was translated into Latin so that copies might be sent for approval to John Calvin, Pierre Viret and Theodore Beza in Geneva, and to Peter Martyr, Heinrich Bullinger and others in Zurich. It was evidently considered premature to submit the work to the Reformation Parliament whose meeting in August 1560 authorized the Confession of Faith, forbade the Mass and annulled papal authority.

In the revision and expansion of the earlier 'Book of Reformation' carried out between August and December 1560 there was some modification and change. The book itself was ready for scrutiny by the General Assembly in December 1560. Its contents confirm that it was examined by an ecclesiastical body and in January 1561 it was presented for approval to a convention of nobles in Edinburgh, where the privy council and many of the nobles present with some qualification consented to the *First Book of Discipline*, the implementation of whose programme became the church's priority.

The *Book of Discipline* aimed at a total 'reformation of religion in the whole realm'. It is illuminated throughout by the genius of Knox and it has left an abiding impression on Scottish religion and life. In the Preface the authors claimed scriptural warrant for their proposals. They recognized the need for preaching the gospel, 'truly and openly in every church throughout the land, the suppression of false teaching and practice imposed on the consciences of men without the expressed commandments of God's Word' (deemed to include saints' days and feast days, obligatory celibacy and distinctive clerical attire). In dealing with the sacraments they insisted that these should be annexed and truly administered 'in such a tongue as the people do understand' (Scots or English) after the manner prescribed in 'the order of Geneva' which was already 'used in some of our churches'. There were two sacraments — baptism and the Lord's Supper. There followed a section, 'Touching the abolition of idolatry', by which was understood 'the Mass, invocation of saints, adoration of images and all honouring of God not contained in his Word'.

In the admission of ministers of the gospel a high standard is set. The candidate is publicly examined, by ministers and elders, for ability to teach and defend the gospel. Ministers are settled in the congregations on election by the people. Where fully qualified ministers are not available readers are to be appointed to read the common prayers and Scripture. The office of reader was an interim provision, until enough ministers for the parishes could be recruited and trained. It is likely that the office of superintendent was designed to be temporary but the plan for it was carefully framed. Ten districts of the country are marked off and referred to as 'dioceses of the superintendents'. These have a recognized relation to the thirteen medieval dioceses. The superintendents were warned not to live like the idle bishops of the past. They were in fact overloaded with work having duties in parishes of their own, together with administration, supervision and travel in their dioceses. Actually only five were appointed, and with their death or retirement, the office was discontinued.

The *Book* lays out the design for a fundamental reform of education. In rural areas the minister or the reader was to teach the children. In every town parish there was to be a schoolmaster. Each town of a superintendent was to have a college with an adequate and well-paid staff. The universities were to be reformed, each according to an elaborate plan that included estimated costs. The patrimony of the church is to be drawn upon for the schools as well as for the support of ministers and the poor. A plea is made, however, for relief from tithes of those 'poor brethren, the labourers and manurers of the ground'. The greed of oppressive landlords and the private seizure of public properties of the church are vigorously condemned.

In the section on the discipline of offenders the secular power is accused of negligence in proceeding against those guilty of blasphemy, adultery, murder and perjury. Among lesser offences, punishable by the church, oppression of the poor is again mentioned; excommunication is the ultimate penalty to be employed only after a series of steps to secure repentance have failed. Excommunication is a grave matter, since it shuts off the offender from business and social life, and the sentence is published through the realm. All are subject to the same discipline, the rulers as well as the ruled.

Explicit directions are given for the conduct of the congregation, including preaching, catechetical instruction, examination for admission to the (quarterly) celebration of the Lord's Supper, prayer and teaching in the home. Once a week in every town 'that exercise that St Paul calleth prophesying' is to be held. The reference is to 1 Corinthians

14:29-31. The Reformers urged the importance of the 'exercise' for the Church of God in Scotland, though with certain cautions against doctrinal error, over-curiosity, and the use of invective in the free discussion. The *Book* also enjoins instruction of children and youth 'especially in the Catechism as we have it now translated in the *Book of Common Order* called the *Order of Geneva*'. In the 'afternoon must the young children be publicly examined in their Catechism in the audience of the people, whereof the minister must take great diligence as well as cause the people to understand the questions proponed as answers', and the doctrines contained therein also.

This radical blueprint was never endorsed by the Scottish Parliament, packed as it was by nobles and lords, but successive General Assemblies of the new kirk stubbornly plugged away and nearly succeeded in creating a nationwide organization that followed the elevated and enlightened aspiration of the *First Book of Discipline*. A *Second Book of Discipline* was published in 1578.

We saw that as far back as 1556 there was an attempt to outline an order for use in the 'Privy Kirks'. With the experience he had in England and in Geneva, Knox's influence was significant. In 1549, during the reign of Edward VI, a *Book of Common Prayer*, largely the work of Cranmer, had been issued and ordered to be read uniformly in the Church of England. In 1552 another edition revised in a Protestant direction was issued. Knox, as we have seen, was responsible for the insertion in the 1552 *Prayer Book* of 'the Black Rubric', explaining that to kneel when receiving the Communion did not imply worshipping the elements. Though Knox did not entirely approve of the book, he recommended its use to his old congregation in Berwick in the interests of unity and peace, and because of the order of the magistrates.

It is likely that the preachers who fled to Scotland from the Marian persecutions brought that *Prayer Book* and therefore the First Covenant drawn up by the Lords of the Congregation in 1557 speaks about 'conforming to the order of the *Book of Common Prayer*'. Meanwhile Knox, as minister of the English exiles in Geneva, with the approval of Calvin and on Calvin's own lines, drew up the *Book of Geneva*. This book made its way to Scotland, and was used here and there by Reformed congregations. Knox's return in 1559 strengthened its position, and in 1562 the General Assembly enjoined the uniform use of it as the *Book of Our Common Order in the administration of the Sacraments and Solemnization of Marriages and Burials of the Dead*. In 1564 a new and enlarged edition was printed in Edinburgh and the Assembly ordered that every minister, exhorter and reader should have a copy and use the *Order* contained within it not only for marriage and the sacraments but also in prayer, thus ousting the hitherto permissible use of the *Second Book of Common Prayer* at ordinary services.

10

SUMMONED BY MARY:

'Madam, in God's presence I speak'

After the Reformation settlement the colleagues of John Knox were eager for him to become one of the new superintendents, agreed upon in the *Book of Discipline*, but he said his health was too poor to undertake the constant travelling. Once Parliament had adopted the Confession of Faith, Knox returned to what he considered his primary duty — the preaching of the gospel and the work of a pastor in a congregation, He was given a salary of £200 a year as minister of St Giles, the highest amount payable to a minister, and the town council agreed to provide him with accommodation. The house he occupied was in Trunk Close, one of the narrow lanes on the north side of the High Street, not far from St Giles.

But Knox's happiness in his new surroundings was all too brief. At the end of November or in early December 1560 he suffered a severe blow with the death of his wife Marjory, leaving him with two sons, aged two and three years. In her last hours she gave her little sons her blessing and prayed that they would always be as true worshippers 'as any that ever sprang out of Abraham's loins'. He gives no information about her death but we know that he felt it keenly. In a letter of condolence Calvin said,

> *You found a wife whose like is not found everywhere, but as you have rightly learned where to seek consolation in sorrow, I am sure that you are bearing this calamity with patience.*

Writing to Goodman, Calvin said,

> *Although I am not little grieved that our brother Knox has been deprived of the most delightful of wives, yet I rejoice that he has not been so afflicted by her death as to cease his active labours in the cause of Christ and the Church.*

It became increasingly clear that what was achieved by Knox and his fellow Reformers in 1560 was going to take a long time to work out both in church and state. The Treaty of Edinburgh might be signed, but it had to be ratified by both England and France. Francois II of France was flatly refusing to have anything to do with it, nor would he ratify the recent legislation regarding the church. There were rumours of the French preparing to send a new army to Scotland and it seemed they were about to disown the Treaty of Edinburgh altogether. Suddenly things changed. Francois II fell ill and died on 5 December 1560, at the age of sixteen. The prospect of Scotland being united to France for ever had dissolved.

The first General Assembly of the Reformed Church met on 20 December 1560. There were forty-two members present, only six of whom were ministers. Knox was one of these. There were thirty-six laymen, presumably elder commissioners from the various established congregations. All the laymen were either burgesses or lairds, none of the nobility being present. At first they had meetings without a leader but as numbers increased and business became more complicated, a moderator was appointed to be chosen at every meeting. They began to initiate action on various matters. The more important steps were those regarding the ordination of more ministers and the appointment of readers. Altogether forty-four men were nominated for these positions. The assembly then drew up a petition to Parliament asking for strict enforcement of the laws against those clergy still celebrating the Mass, and naming those who it knew to be offenders. It also decided to hold future assemblies twice a year.

Meeting in Edinburgh on 15 January 1561 the Protestant leaders instructed Lord James Stewart to go to France and ask Mary to return to Scotland. They might not like her religion but she was their Queen and the Lords had persuaded themselves that she would listen to advice and convert to Protestantism. Before he left, Lord James took the precaution of speaking to John Knox, for Mary had indicated that she would not set foot in Scotland as long as Knox was there. Knox was prevailed upon to produce some written undertaking not to stir up the Scots to rebel against their female ruler. On the other hand, Knox and the Lords of the Congregation insisted to Lord James that on no account must he agree to the Mass being said in Scotland, either publicly or privately. Mary refused to become a Protestant but she was prepared to go back to Scotland provided she was allowed to attend her own private Catholic services. Lord James agreed, on condition that she would recognize the Protestant Church.

At the same meeting the Convention turned their attention to some other matters which had remained unresolved while Francis II was alive. It was important that a properly organized church should be set up to carry on the work of reformation by implementing the recommendations of the *Book of Discipline.* For six days the Convention debated whether they should agree to the plan presented by Knox and his colleagues. A number were opposed to it. Some of the Lords feared that they would lose much of the land that they had seized. On 27 January a good many nobles and lairds signed a statement accepting the *Book of Discipline* with the proviso that those who held benefices should continue to hold them for life, while paying the minister's salaries out of the revenues.

Meanwhile in France, Mary asked Elizabeth I of England for safe conduct for her voyage to Scotland, in case storms drove her ashore on the east coast of England. Elizabeth, conscious that Mary had not ratified the Treaty of Edinburgh, refused. Undeterred, Mary set sail in her great white galley on 14 August 1561, and five days later arrived in Leith in dense fog about eight o'clock in the morning. She received a warm welcome and was ceremoniously escorted to Holyrood House that afternoon. In the evening folk gathered beneath her windows to serenade her with psalms, while bonfires lit up the darkened sky.

Knox was not so ready to welcome her. He declared: 'The very face of heaven the time of her arrival did manifestly speak what comfort was brought into this country with her, to wit, sorrow, dolour, darkness and all impiety.' In less than a week his worst fears seemed to be confirmed when he heard that preparations were being made to hold Mass at Holyrood on Sunday 24 August. Protestants came to object and, fearing a riot, Lord James stood guard on the chapel door. When he was asked what he was doing there he replied that he was making sure that no Scotsman attended the Roman Catholic service. The Privy Council met to discuss the matter and decided that they would not object to Mass being said at Holyrood.

On the first Sunday after the Mass was said, Knox preached against it to a large congregation in St Giles. That one Mass, he said, was more fearful to him than if ten thousand armed enemies had landed. Mary summoned Knox to appear before her at Holyrood and so it was that on 4 September 1561 he marched down to the Palace. The Queen spoke first, making four accusations against him. He had raised a number of his subjects against her mother Mary of Guise and against herself; he had written a book against her authority (*The First Blast*); he had caused great sedition and slaughter in England; and, she had heard, he had done all that by means of necromancy.

Knox replied by saying he had taught people only the truth. He readily admitted having written *The First Blast*, and if anyone would disprove the arguments in it, then he would willingly confess his error. Provided she did not persecute Protestants then neither he, nor *The First Blast*, would do her any harm. He pointed out that it had been aimed specifically at that wicked Jezebel of England, Mary Tudor. He had certainly not stirred up sedition in England. Berwick had never been so peaceful as during his stay there. Those who accused him of dabbling in the black arts were slandering him, as anyone who had heard him preach could testify.

Mary persisted and claimed he had taught the people to receive another religion than their princes could allow.

Madam (said he) as right religion took neither original strength nor authority from worldly Princes, but from the eternal God alone, so are not subjects bound to frame their religion according to the appetites of the Princes.

She questioned how can that doctrine be of God, seeing that God commands subjects to obey their princes? The reply from Knox was that princes were often the most ignorant of true religion. 'Think ye that subjects having the power may resist their princes?' Mary asked. Knox replied that just as children would be justified in binding and imprisoning their father if he tried to kill them so were subjects justified in restraining and incarcerating a prince who sought to murder the children of God. The interview ended when a servant came to summon Mary to dinner. Knox concluded: 'I pray God, Madam, that ye may be as blessed within the Commonwealth of Scotland, if it be the pleasure of God, as ever Deborah was in the Commonwealth of Israel.'

In the faith of the unprepossessing little preacher, scarcely up to her shoulder in height, Mary met a rock she could neither move nor soften. In the tall charming young widow Knox discerned: 'If there be not in her a proud mind, a crafty wit, and an indurate heart against God and his truth, my judgment faileth me.' A few weeks later he repeated his verdict on her in a letter to William Cecil: 'In communications with her I espied such craft as I have not found in such age.'

Knox became quite depressed over the way things were going. Writing to Anne Locke on 2 October 1561, he said, 'Remedy there appeareth none, unless we would arm the hands of the people in whom abideth yet some sparks of God's fear,' but he had no real intention of stirring up the 'rascal' multitude and he added that he longed for death. In early November 1561 a meeting was held in the house of the Lord Clerk Register to discuss the problem of Mary's Mass. Knox and some of the other preachers who were there were of the opinion that subjects were entitled 'to suppress the idolatry of their prince', but the majority were of the view that no one could lawfully forbid the Queen to have her Roman Catholic services.

In December some provision was made at last for the Protestant ministers. The Archbishop of St Andrews and three of the Roman Catholic bishops had offered to give the Queen a quarter of their revenues for one year. On 15 February 1562 the Privy Council issued an act stating that a third of all ecclesiastical revenues were to be surrendered to the crown. Half would be used for the Protestant preacher's salaries and Mary would keep the other half for her own household expenditure. Knox's assessment was: 'I see two parts fully given to the devil and the third must be divided between God and the devil.' The sum collected was not nearly enough to fund all the Protestant pastors.

Knox kept a close watch on everything that Mary Queen of Scots was doing and in December he heard that, on receiving news of a Roman Catholic victory in France, she danced for joy until after midnight. It was a false rumour. On 13 December 1562, Knox preached a sermon against the ignorance and vanity of princes, criticizing in particular Mary's love for dancing. As soon as the Queen heard about it she sent for him, and on Tuesday 15 December he made his way down to Holyrood for his second audience with her. Mary embarked on a long speech accusing Knox of having spoken of her irreverently and of trying to make her subjects hate and despise her. His reply was:

*I am called, Madam, to a public function within the Kirk
of God and am appointed by God to rebuke the sins and
vices of all. I am not appointed to come to every man in
particular to show him his offence, for that labour were
infinite.*

As Knox left, Catholic courtiers who saw his cheerful
countenance asked him why he was not afraid. 'Why should
the pleasing face of a gentlewoman frighten me?' he replied.
'I have looked in the face of many angry men and yet have
not been afraid above measure.'

A few days later, on 25 December, the General Assembly
convened again in Edinburgh. There were three important
matters concerning Knox. The first was the care of the poor
and he was authorized to prepare and present a petition to
the Queen. Another was securing better living conditions for
the ministers by having the manses and glebes (land) of their
churches turned over to them. Third, the Assembly agreed
that the *Book of Geneva* was to be used for the services of the
sacraments, marriages and burials. Communion was to be
held four times a year in urban areas and twice a year in rural
parishes. Although in the *Book of Discipline* the Genevan
liturgy had been taken for granted, it now officially became
the *Book Of Common Order.* It was not to be regarded as
a prayer book and the worship services on the Lord's Day
were conducted according to the discretion of the minister.

As the General Assembly was seeking to establish the
Reformed worship the Roman Catholic element, led by
Archbishop John Hamilton, was trying to re-establish
the Mass. At Easter 1563 various priests in the west of
Scotland took it on themselves to observe the Mass,
contrary to the law, and for this they were arrested by the

local Protestant lairds. When Mary heard this she was angered and summoned Knox to Lochleven, where she was hunting. This was his third audience with the Queen. She spent some time trying to make him promise to persuade the gentlemen of the west not to punish anyone for their religious observances. He replied that he could promise that there would be quietness throughout the country if she punished wrongdoers according to the law. If she did not do so, he feared that there were those who would take the law into their own hands: 'The sword of justice, Madam, is God's and is given to rulers and princes for one end.' In Scotland judges were empowered by an Act of Parliament to seek out and punish those who celebrated Mass and he told her that it was her duty to support them.

As Parliament was about to convene soon after Hamilton's attempt to revive the Mass, awkward questions might be asked if Mary did nothing to enforce the anti-Catholic laws. She therefore brought to trial the Archbishop and his forty-seven supporters, whom, when they were found guilty, she imprisoned during the meeting of Parliament. Nothing was done to ratify the legislation establishing Protestantism in Scotland or the Treaty of Edinburgh. Mary had maintained that the Acts of the 1560 Parliament were illegal. She had accordingly persuaded Lord James Stewart, Earl of Moray, not to raise the question of the religious settlement in Parliament. Instead the Protestant Lords begged her to grant an act of oblivion to all who had been involved in the recent civil war. Knox was bitterly angry with the Lords who had deliberately let the opportunity pass them by. He felt betrayed, and after he and Moray quarrelled fiercely they did not speak to each other for another eighteen months.

At this time Knox preached to a large congregation reminding them of God's past mercies and criticizing their ingratitude. 'Shall this be the thankfulness ye shall render unto your God? To betray his cause, when ye have it in your hands to establish it as you please.' He turned to rumours about the Queen's marriage. She had many suitors who were Roman Catholics. He said that if the Lords consented to her marriage with an infidel, 'and all papists are infidels', then they would be banishing Jesus Christ from the realm. The Queen was bitterly upset. She summoned him to appear before her for the fourth time.

He was not long in her presence when she burst into tears. After Knox explained his position as one sent to preach the Word, she continued: 'What have ye to do with my marriage? Or what are ye within this commonwealth?' It brought a reply from Knox which has become famous:

A subject born within the same, Madam. And albeit I neither be Earl, Lord or Baron within it, yet God has made me (however abject that ever I be in your eyes) a profitable member within the same.

He warned her of the danger to the commonwealth of a Roman Catholic and Spanish alliance. Hearing this, Mary broke into sobbing again. Knox waited for what to him seemed 'a long season' until he was forced to say:

Madam, in God's presence I speak. I never delighted in the weeping of any of God's creatures, yea I can scarcely well abide the tears of my own boys whom my hand corrects, much less can I rejoice in your Majesty's weeping.

11

THE LAST CALL:

'Now it is come'

Knox was now nearing the age of fifty. His sons were growing up and his mother-in-law Mrs Bowes was elderly and could not expect to run his household for ever. He found a new wife in Margaret Stewart, daughter of Lord Ochiltree. They married on Sunday 25 March 1564, when Margaret was just seventeen. Mary was furious that Knox dared to marry someone of her own family, the royal house of Stewart. After the wedding Knox decided to send his two sons to the safety of England to be educated under the supervision of their Bowes relatives. Towards the end of 1565 the first child of his second marriage was born and was named Martha.

Meanwhile Mary Queen of Scots was still pursuing the Spanish connection. Knox was not alone in seeing the prospect of a Spanish marriage as a dire threat to Protestantism and the commonwealth. However, at last the Spanish match fell through, when on 6 August 1564, Philip II announced that his negotiations with the Scots

were at an end. However, events took a turn for the worse
and in the next year the polarization and conflict between
the Protestant and Roman Catholic elements became radical
and violent. The next prospect of marriage for Mary was with
Henry, Lord Darnley. He could claim to be, next to Mary,
heir to the English throne by right of descent. She believed
such a marriage would strengthen her hand in Scotland and
also her claim to the English throne. At first some seemed
to think that Darnley was a Protestant but he soon indicated
the error of such a view. There was growing opposition to the
marriage. Mary issued a proclamation promising, in return
for consent to the marriage, to preserve the Protestant
religion and the privileges of the Reformed Church.

Knox strongly opposed the marriage as the beginning
of the overthrow of Protestantism in Scotland. He realized
that Mary was playing a double game despite all her
proclamations of tolerance. Mary and Darnley were married
on 29 July 1565, according to Roman Catholic rites. On
Sunday 19 August Mary sent Darnley to St Giles to listen
to the preaching of Knox. In a sermon on Isaiah 26:13-21
the preacher spoke of all political authority being derived
from God and warned his hearers against those who would
persecute the faithful church. At one point he declared that
God punished sinful people by putting boys and women
to rule over them. Darnley was furious and complained to
the Privy Council. Knox was summoned before them and
ordered to refrain from preaching as long as the royal couple
were in the burgh. The Edinburgh Burgh Council stood
against this decision and resolved about Knox that they 'will
no manner of way consent or grant that his mouth be closed'.

Mary's efforts to re-establish Roman Catholicism was
encouraged by her new secretary, the Italian David Riccio,

who had recently come to Scotland. Many of the Protestants regarded him as a papal emissary. Darnley and the nobles were opposed to him and conspired to murder him in Holyrood on 9 March 1566. Mary was in active pursuit of his murderers but this came to a halt because she was with child and on 19 June a son was born, the future James VI. Believing that the prime culprit in the Riccio murder was her husband Darnley, in December 1566 she pardoned the others involved. She then became infatuated with the young and handsome James, Earl of Bothwell. The Earl had no qualms of conscience about removing Darnley by any means, and so, on 9 February 1567, the House at Kirk o' Field was blown up and Darnley was strangled. Bothwell carried Mary off to Dunbar Castle and married her according to Protestant rites. There was great indignation over this, with the result that Bothwell fled to the North and Mary surrendered to the opposition. She was imprisoned in Lochleven Castle and forced to sign an instrument of abdication in favour of her young son James, and to confer the regency on the Earl of Moray.

When these events were taking place John Knox was in the North of England visiting his sons and no doubt members of his former congregations. He returned home in June and immediately raised his voice against Mary, demanding that she suffer the death penalty for adultery and murder. In this he was supported by the rank and file of the Protestant population. The General Assembly met at the end of June but postponed action until more lords and burgesses could attend. The result was a large gathering on 20 July in which Knox took an active part. The assembly proceeded to draw a series of articles which it hoped the Parliament would ratify in order to finally establish the church. Knox had made up his quarrel with the Earl of Moray and he preached the sermon at the coronation of James VI in Stirling on 31 July.

The Parliament met at the beginning of December under the Earl of Moray. Knox preached at the opening, and, as in 1560, it was the most fully attended in years. Bothwell was condemned for the murder of the king. Then the Acts of 1560 concerning the church, which Mary had never ratified, were once again brought forward and passed with the approval of the Regent. When the Parliament concluded, the Reformed Kirk was at last established by law within the land. In all of this Knox played an important part right to the end. He could look with a measure of satisfaction on a work accomplished, but he knew that the struggle was destined to go on.

In the subsequent days Knox lived in the dread of Mary regaining the throne. His fears were justified when on 2 May 1568, Mary escaped from Lochleven Castle. She rode west to Hamilton to gather her supporters and marched against the Regent Moray. They met at Langside and the Queen's forces were quickly routed. Convinced that Elizabeth would support her against her rebellious subjects she fled to England. On 2 January 1570, Knox warned Cecil: 'If ye strike not at the roots, the branches that appear to be broken will bud again (and that more quickly than men can believe) with greater force than we would wish.' In a mood of gloomy foreboding he signed himself 'John Knox with his one foot in the grave'. He was hearing of plots to murder Moray and sent him warnings but Moray ignored his advice. Three weeks later Moray was assassinated as he rode out of Linlithgow. At the funeral service in St Giles on 14 February there were 3,000 present and Knox reduced the audience to tears with a description of the Regent's virtues. The successor to Moray was the Earl of Lennox. By this time the struggle between James VI supporters and those of Mary, Queen of Scots, had degenerated to civil war with the King's Party fighting the Queen's Party.

In the autumn of 1570 Knox suffered a stroke and for a few days he lost the power of speech. Although his enemies declared that God had struck him dumb for his sins, before long he was back preaching. He later said that he had been half-dead since the illness, and it is possible he suffered permanent weakness on one side. Besides this, Knox was living in dangerous circumstances. He suffered a blow when Kirkcaldy of Grange, his good friend and ally from St Andrews Castle days, changed sides. Moray had appointed him Captain of Edinburgh Castle and when he declared for Mary's side Knox said,

To see stars fall from heaven and a man of knowledge commit so manifest a treason what godly heart cannot but lament, tremble and fear.

Knox continued to be outspoken against the Queen. The King's Party captured Dumbarton Castle held by the Hamiltons for the Queen. Archbishop Hamilton was taken out and hanged at Stirling on 7 April 1571. His supporters fled to Edinburgh and joined Kirkcaldy in the Castle. With so many of the enemy at hand Knox's friends feared for his life. On 30 April Kirkcaldy issued a proclamation ordering all supporters of the King's Party to leave Edinburgh within six hours.

Although reluctant to leave at first, Knox was persuaded to go and on 5 May he and his wife and their three small girls (his third daughter Elizabeth had been born the previous year), along with his secretary Richard Bannatyne, left the house in Trunk Close and crossed the Forth to Abbotshall, near Kirkcaldy. In July 1571 they travelled slowly to St Andrews where he and his household lodged near St Leonard's College. He was so frail that he expected to die in St Andrews where he had been first called into the work of the ministry. Even so, he preached whenever he could and James Melville, then a fifteen-year-old student, was to describe how he used to see Knox walking slowly to church wearing a long robe with furs round his neck and leaning heavily on a stick with his right hand, while his faithful secretary, Richard Bannatyne, supported him on the left side with a hand under his armpit.

> *Of all the benefits I had that year, was the coming among us of that most notable prophet and apostle of our nation, Mr. John Knox, to St. Andrews. I heard him teach there the prophecies of Daniel. In the opening up of his text he was moderate the space of a half-hour; but when he entered to application, he made me so to grew [quake] and tremble, that I could not hold a pen to write ... he was 'lifted up to the pulpit, where he behoved to lean at his first entry, but before he had done with his sermon, he was so active and vigorous, that he was like to ding [smash] that pulpit in blads [pieces] and fly out of it'. Mr. Knox would sometime come in and repose himself in our college-yard, and call us scholars to him and bless us, and exhort us to know God and His work in our country, and stand by the good cause.*

On 31 July 1572, a truce was agreed between the Regent's forces and that of Queen Mary. Knox received messages from some of the congregation at St Giles urging him to return to Edinburgh. That August Knox and his family arrived in Leith and after a few days went on to Edinburgh where they were lodged in the house of a goldsmith by the name of Mossman (the present John Knox's House), hard by the Netherbow. He was 'now so feeble as scarce can he stand alone'. Despite his ill health he attempted to carry on his preaching as before, but his voice was so weak it could be heard by only a few who were close to the pulpit. It was agreed that he should move to a much smaller building attached to St Giles, known as the Outer Tolbooth. He preached there as often as he was able, dwelling on the theme on which he had long wished to close his ministry — the sufferings and death of Christ.

In early September news reached Scotland of the Massacre of St Bartholomew's Day in France on 24 August. Tens of thousands of French Protestants were murdered on the orders of the French king, Charles IX. Summoning up his strength Knox thundered forth the vengeance of heaven against 'that cruel murderer the king of France' and ordered Le Croc, the French ambassador, to go and tell his master that sentence was pronounced against him in Scotland and that divine vengeance would never depart from him or his house unless they repented.

In view of his increasing weakness, the necessity for a successor became more urgent. The choice fell on James Lawson of Aberdeen to whom Knox wrote on 7 September inviting him to Edinburgh to preach, with the urgent postscript: 'Make haste my brother, otherwise you will come too late'. Lawson responded immediately and after preaching a number of times before the congregation, he was called to be their minister. Knox's last appearance in the pulpit was on 9 November 1572. After preaching in the Tolbooth he went into St Giles where he took part in the induction of his successor James Lawson. He preached the sermon in which he pointed out the mutual duties of minister and congregation, and closed with a fervent prayer for divine blessing on both minister and the congregation. After that, 'leaning upon his staff and the arm of an attendant', he crept down the street which was lined with the audience, who, as if anxious to take the last sight of their beloved pastor, followed him until he entered his house from which he never came out alive.

The next day he was afflicted with a violent cough which further weakened him. On Friday 14 November, he rose from his bed sooner than his usual hour, and thinking it was the Sabbath he said that he meant to go to church and preach on the resurrection of Christ, upon which he had meditated through the whole night. The next day when two of his friends, John Durie and Archibald Stewart, came to the house not knowing he was so sick, he rose and persuaded them to stay for dinner. He sat at the table for the last time. He ordered a hogshead of wine which was in the cellar to be pierced and asked Archibald Stewart to send for some of it as long as it lasted, for he would not tarry until it was all drunk.

On Monday 17 November, he met with his colleagues to leave them his dying charge. James Lawson, the elders and deacons, and David Lindsay, one of the ministers of Leith, assembled in his room when he addressed them the following words:

The day approaches and is now before the door, for which I have frequently and vehemently thirsted, when I shall be released from my great labours and innumerable sorrows, and shall be with Christ. And now God is my witness, whom I served in the spirit in the Gospel of his Son, that I have taught nothing but the true and solid doctrine of the Gospel of the Son of God, and have had it only for my object to instruct the ignorant, to confirm the faithful, to comfort the weak, the fearful and the distressed, by the promises of grace, and to fight against the proud and the rebellious by the divine threatenings.

I know that many have complained much and loudly, and do still complain of my too great severity; but God knows that my mind was always free from hatred to the persons of those against whom I denounced the heavy judgments of God. In the meantime, I cannot deny but I felt the greatest abhorrence of the sin in which they indulged still, however, keeping this one thing in view, that if it were possible, I might gain them to the Lord. But a certain reverential fear of my God who called me, and was pleased of his grace to make me a steward of divine mysteries, to whom I knew I must render an account, when I shall appear before his tribunal, of the manner in which I have discharged the embassy which he committed to me — had such a powerful effect as to make me utter so intrepidily whatever the Lord put into my mouth, without any respect of persons. Therefore, I profess before God and his holy angels, that I never made gain of the sacred word of God, that I never studied to please men, never indulged in my own private passions or those of others, but faithfully distributed the talent entrusted to my care for the edification of the church over which I did watch.

Over the next three days, although he could not speak without great pain he continued to receive persons of every rank. On Friday 21 November, he asked Richard Bannatyne to order his coffin, and spent much of that day in meditation and prayer.

Come, Lord Jesus, Sweet Jesus, into thy hands I commend my spirit. Be merciful Lord to Thy Church which thou hast redeemed. Give peace to this afflicted commonwealth. Raise up faithful pastors who will take charge of thy Church. Grant us, Lord, the perfect hatred of sin, both by the evidence of Thy wrath and mercy.

On Sunday 23 November, during the afternoon sermon, he had been lying quiet for a considerable time when he suddenly exclaimed:

I have been these last two nights in meditation of the troubled Church of God, the spouse of Jesus Christ, despised of the world but precious in his sight. I have called to God for her, and have committed her to her Head, Jesus Christ. I have been fighting against Satan, who is ever ready to assault; yea, I have fought against spiritual wickedness in heavenly things and have prevailed. I have been in heaven and have possession, and have tasted of those heavenly joys where presently I am.

The following day Knox insisted on rising and getting dressed, but after only half an hour of sitting in a chair he had to go back to bed again. It was evident that his end was drawing near. Besides his wife and Richard Bannatyne, three close friends waited by his bedside. Mr Campbell of Kinyeancleugh asked him if he had any pain, to which he replied: 'It is no painful pain, but such a pain as shall soon, I trust, put an end to the battle.' He continued: 'I must leave the care of my wife and children to you to whom you must be a husband in my room.' About three o'clock in the afternoon he asked his wife to read to him from 1 Corinthians 15. 'Is not that a comfortable chapter?' he said, when it was finished. About five o'clock he told his wife: 'Go read where I first cast my anchor', upon which she read John 17.

After that he went to sleep for a while during which he uttered heavy groans. When he awoke and was asked the cause of his sighing so deeply he replied:

I have indeed formerly sustained many contests in this frail life, and many assaults from Satan; but at this time that roaring lion hath most furiously attacked me and put forth all his strength, that he might devour and make an end of me at once. Often before hath he placed my sins before my eyes; often tempted me to despair; often endeavoured to entangle me with the allurements of the world; but these weapons, being broken by the sword of the Spirit, which is the Word of God, he could accomplish nothing. But now he has attacked me in another way; for the cunning serpent has endeavoured to persuade me that I have merited heaven itself, and a blessed immortality by the faithful discharge of the ministerial office committed to me. But, blessed be God, who suggested to me those passages of Scripture by which I was able to grapple with him, and extinguish this fiery dart; among which were these: 'What hast thou that thou hast not received?'; and, 'By the grace of God I am what I am'; and, 'Not I, but the grace of God in me.' And thus vanquished, he went away; wherefore I give thanks to my God by Jesus Christ, who was pleased to grant me the victory; and I am persuaded that the tempter shall not again attack me, but within a short time, I shall, without any great bodily pain, or

anguish of mind, exchange this mortal and miserable life for
a blessed immortality through Jesus Christ.

He then lay quiet for some hours. At ten o'clock they read the evening prayers. His doctor bent over him to ask if he could hear the prayers and he answered: 'I would to God that you and all men had heard them as I have heard them; praise God for that heavenly sound.' About eleven o'clock he commended himself to God, gave a deep sigh and said, 'Now it is come.' Richard Bannatyne desired him to think upon those comfortable promises of our Saviour Jesus Christ which he had so often declared to others. Perceiving he was speechless, he asked him to give a sign that he had heard them and would die in peace. Upon this, he lifted up one of his hands, and sighing twice, expired without a struggle. The words of his faithful secretary sum up his life and death:

In this manner departed this man of God: the light of Scotland, the comfort of the Church within the same, the mirror of godliness, and pattern and example of all true ministers, in purity of life, soundness in doctrine, and boldness in reproving of wickedness: one who cared not the favour of men, how great soever they were. What dexterity in teaching, boldness in reproving, and hatred of wickedness was in him, my ignorant dulness is not able to declare, which if I could preis [labour] to set out, it were one who would light a candle to let men see the sun; seeing all his virtues are better known and notified to the world a thousand fold than I am able to express.

Two days later he was buried in the graveyard to the south of St Giles Kirk. His remains were conveyed to the last resting place by the Earl of Morton, the newly elected regent, and by the Lords and Commons. As they closed the grave, the Earl declared: 'There lies he who never feared nor flattered any flesh.' This epitaph coming from such a ruthless figure speaks volumes concerning Knox.

At the time of his death his wife Margaret was about twenty-four and all three daughters, Martha, Margaret and Elizabeth, were under the age of eight. After two years his widow Margaret married Andrew Ker, a widower in his forties, and a strong Protestant.

Knox's widow and three daughters were his executors. The total value of his estate was £1,528. To his sons by Marjory Bowes, Nathaniel and Eleazer, he left £500 along with some silver plate and £30 worth of his books. Eight days after his death the sons entered St John's College, Cambridge. Nathaniel became Fellow of the College but died in his early twenties. Eleazer was a vicar in the Church of England in Essex, dying on 22 May 1591, at the age of thirty-three.

Of Knox's three daughters, Margaret and Elizabeth married eminent Church of Scotland ministers, Zachary Pont and John Welsh. Welsh opposed James VI's ecclesiastical policies and spent sixteen years in exile in France. It is said that Elizabeth went on one occasion to the king to seek permission for her husband to return. This was the daughter of John Knox confronting the son of Mary Queen of Scots. When Elizabeth explained her request the king asked her the name of her father. On hearing who it was, the king exclaimed: 'Knox and Welsh! The devil never made such a match as that.' Elizabeth retorted with her father's fearlessness and humour: 'It is right likely, Sire, for we never asked his advice.'

12

THE KNOX LEGACY

John Knox is one of the most controversial figures in Scottish history. He is often remembered for the wrong reasons, such as his treatise, *The First Blast of the Trumpet against the Monstrous Regiment of Women,* the riots in Perth, or his conflicts with Mary, Queen of Scots. It is doubtful if any figure in Scottish church history has been demonized to the same extent. His fiercest critics have been those who had no sympathy with his theology. They have tended to focus on certain aspects of his character. Knox admitted that 'of nature I am churlish' and he knew that he was tactless. There was quite a contrast between his sensitivity and his vehement denunciation of anyone of whom he disapproved. However he had the stamp of a prophet about him and what he accomplished in his life, and the legacy he left behind, far outweighs these other considerations.

He was the man suited to the hour

Martin Luther put forward the idea that whenever God means to work decisively in his church he raises a wonder-man (Wundermann), a hero, a great individual leader to be his instrument. This was certainly true in Scotland. Knox bestrode the kingdom like a colossus. He was a man suited for the challenge of the times. We see the wisdom of providence in raising up a person with the qualities suited to the work allotted him. The talents which a person has for acting with usefulness in one age and situation, would render him wholly unsuitable for another. John the Baptist, the austere prophet in the wilderness, was the way-preparer for the Messiah 'who did not strive nor cry nor cause his voice to be heard in the streets'. Before the Reformation, superstition fed by spiritual ignorance, and armed with power, governed Scotland with a gigantic sway. A man of mild spirits and gentle manners would have been as unfit for taking the field against the enemy, as a child would be for encountering a giant. As William Robertson said of Knox, 'Those very qualities which now render his character less amiable fitted him to be the instrument of providence for advancing the Reformation among a fierce people, and enabled him to face danger, and surmount opposition, from which men of a more gentle spirit would have been apt to shrink back.'

The fear of God motivated his life and work

The outstanding strength and courage shown by John Knox arose from a strong sense of the presence of God in his life. At the heart of his Christian experience was a vision of God on his throne. Like Calvin, his great mentor, he lived *coram Deo*, before the face of God. It was the relentless orientation on the glory of God which gave coherence to his doctrine and to his life. His conviction could best be expressed in the words of the prophet Elijah, 'As the Lord, the God of Israel, lives, before whom I stand.' In a climactic moment at Holyrood in the presence of Mary, Queen of Scots, he exclaimed: 'Madam, in God's presence I speak.' It was this fear of God in him that banished the fear of man. When we consider his reticence in responding to the call of the congregation in the castle at St Andrews we have to conclude that the bravery must have been God-given and not merely constitutional.

His first and main calling was a preacher of the Word

The charge of the Reformers against the system that preceded them was that it failed to bring men into the presence of God. Calvin's view was that if there was to be a meeting between a holy God and man in his desperately sinful condition this meeting must take place in the preaching of the Word. Everywhere the Reformation made an impact, particularly in Scotland, it did so by the production and proliferation of translations of the Scriptures and the verbal proclamation of the Word of God. Knox regarded the Roman system as idolatrous and destructive of the souls of men. He believed that he was called 'to blow the Master's trumpet', as the Israelites did when they blew the trumpets marching round the walls of Jericho, to bring the system down.

Preaching was that in which he delighted and for which he was qualified by undoubted gifts and extensive knowledge of Scripture. He had the art of applying the Word to the existing circumstances of the church. His powers of alarming the conscience and arousing the passions were greatly used. As a result of a Word-based Reformation the preaching of the Word has had a distinctive importance in the worship of the Scottish Church, and has enriched many generations of Scottish people with a liberal education in the highest and deepest matters. It is to Knox and to those who laboured with him that we must trace this coronation of the pulpit and the sermon in the Scottish Church.

He was constrained to be a Reformer

The whole conflict of the Scottish Reformation was, as Knox constantly affirmed, 'a battle' against the rage of Satan. The Reformers knew that there was an enemy whose great aim was to silence the voice of the gospel. That was what brought about the martyrdoms of Hamilton and Wishart. Therefore the Scottish Reformation had its destructive as well as its constructive side. There was a great and entrenched mass of superstitions, which it must drive from the land and from the souls of men. Nobody set about the task of expulsion with more zeal than John Knox. If it were not for the resolution and courage of Knox the whole movement might have failed. He was the one person who seemed capable of maintaining and strengthening the morale of the forces that were seeking to make the Reformation successful. He was able to keep his faith and stimulate those who were wavering to action and achievement.

His call to do so was similar to that of the prophet Jeremiah: 'Behold I have put thy words in thy mouth. See

I have this day set thee over the nations and the kingdoms, to root out, and to pull down, and to destroy, and to throw down, to build and to plant.' For the dogmas and practices of the Roman Church — transubstantiation, papistical indulgences, purgatory, pilgrimages, praying to departed saints — he had not a particle of tolerance. Sometimes his contempt was withering, and his sarcasm couched in language which later generations may have pronounced as over-rough. From the time that he embraced the Reformed doctrines the desire of propagating them and of delivering his country from the delusions and corruptions of popery became his ruling passion, to which he was always willing to sacrifice his ease, his interest, his reputation and his life.

He created the Scottish Church on the Geneva pattern

The Reformers were all agreed that the Medieval Church was no longer a gathering of the faithful, but a worldly institution whose status derived from the authority and traditions of men and external connection with clergy, sacraments and buildings. The restoration of the centrality of Christ in salvation meant the recovery of the priesthood of all believers. In unison with Luther, Calvin and Zwingli, Knox shattered the barriers which divided the common man from God; and he published the good news that access to the 'holiest of all' is no exclusive privilege of the priest, but the glad prerogative of each sinful and needy and thirsting heart. The special power of the ordained priesthood was broken and every believer could now come to enjoy the privileges of priesthood. The new teaching freed the land from priestcraft, with all its attendant evils. It freed Scotland from the curse of clericalism. The absolute authority of the church over the souls of men and women was at an end.

It was Knox who shaped what manner of polity and government the church of Scotland ought to have. The rights of all the members were readily acknowledged, and their responsibilities were effectively taught. He laid the groundwork for the later establishment of a truly Presbyterian church under Andrew Melville. His influence shows in the 'Covenanting' movement of the seventeenth century. That spirit of resistance to state interference in the church and insistence on the rights of congregations continued on in Scotland in the following centuries. In particular, Knox made the General Assembly the true Parliament and Legislature of Scotland. Writing in 1905, Alexander Smellie said, 'If the Kirk has been, since the days of the Reformation, the chiefest and sublimest entity in our Scottish realm, watching sedulously over the best interests of the commonwealth, reproving public sin and contending for public godliness, speaking on the people's behalf with a voice that was truer than that of any tyrant on the throne, gaining and conserving and advancing the liberties of the land, it was Knox who, under God, invested the Kirk with such sacredness and majesty.'

He laid foundations for the future state

As well as modelling the church in Scotland, Knox laid the foundation of an extraordinary forward-looking new state, way ahead of the time in such matters as education, social welfare and democracy. The Reformation had its effect in all spheres of national life. Knox roused the common man to a sense of his true dignity. He said, 'Before God all men are equal. In matters of religion God requires no less of the subject, be he ever so poor, than of the prince and the rich man.'

Educationally the Reformation gave a great impetus to literacy as the common people learned to read the Bible for themselves. Knox brought forward the first comprehensive scheme of national education, where every parish would have a schoolmaster and every notable town a college, and where the children of the poor would have their education free. The importance of education became a basic characteristic of the Scots both at home and abroad.

Socially it broke down the wall between the sacred and the secular, leading to a fresh appreciation of marriage, family and the divine calling of everyday work. It has been said that no philanthropist, no socialist of them all, has championed the cause of the poor more manfully and more lovingly than Knox did. His concept of the responsibility of the church for the care of the poor as outlined in the *Book of Discipline* was maintained into the nineteenth century, revealing itself in the work of Thomas Chalmers, Thomas Guthrie and James Begg.

It is in his influence on the political front that opinion about Knox is divided. He believed in the right of subjects to revolt against their rulers. It was when faced with the tyranny and persecution of Mary Tudor that he began to question the relationship of the people to the ruler. Along with other Marian exiles in Switzerland he wrestled with the problem and was influenced by the teaching of Heinrich Bullinger, whose views were based on the principle of the sovereignty of law, and the conception that absolute monarchy is contrary to universal rules of right supposed to underlie all government.

Knox held that a king does not rule over a Christian people by birth only. In the election of a ruler the ordinance of God for the appointment for magistrates must be observed. No manifest idolater should be given public office in a kingdom that has once acknowledged Jesus Christ. If people have elected a ruler who turns out to be an idolater, those who did the electing may remove and punish him. As we noted in the interview with Mary, Queen of Scots, in September 1561, Knox maintained that just as children would be justified in binding and imprisoning their father if he tried to kill them, so were subjects justified in restraining and incarcerating a prince who sought to murder the children of God. In his *Story of the Scottish Reformation*, Alexander Renwick commented on Knox's opinion in that interview, saying, 'He expressed views far ahead of his time, and was declaring in essence that doctrine of limited monarchy under which our country has thrived so remarkably.'

He 'made Scotland over again in his own image'

It is given to few men to shape a generation but Knox, in Thomas Carlyle's phrase, 'made Scotland over again in his own image'. Throughout the long dark centuries which covered medieval Europe the common man was, inevitably, politically passive. It was servitude from cradle to grave. He was taught by 'the king his father' and by 'the Church his mother' that he was, with his fellows, a member of a great 'body politic' where only the head could rule — and where the lesser members must dutifully obey. Carlyle spoke of pre-Reformation Scotland as a country without a soul but the change was such that,

*at the Reformation the internal life is kindled, as it were,
under the ribs of this outward, material death ... this that
Knox did for his nation we may really call a resurrection as
from death ... the people began to live.*

Dr Hume Brown has said that, 'previous to the great
religious conflict, there never was an issue before the
Scottish people that went deep enough to elicit the instincts
and tendencies which must be awakened before what we
call a nation becomes possible'. The Reformation, he tells us,
even more than the War of Independence, first gave birth to
the civic and corporate life of our land. This, too, is part of
the debt under which we lie to John Knox. It led Sir William
Stirling Maxwell to say, 'No man in England or Scotland
who values liberty, national, civil or religious, can speak of
Knox without reverence and gratitude.'

Appendix

Political background to Knox's time

To help understand the factors that influenced the progress of the Reformation under John Knox it might be helpful to look at the political background of the times.

The relations of Scotland and England during the Middle Ages were, normally, hostile. English kings attempted to reduce Scotland to vassalage, while the Scottish rulers contended for full national autonomy. France was the natural ally of England's northern enemy, and the 'auld alliance' was maintained even after it became burdensome to the Scots. Henry VII (1485-1509) planned an end of the feud with Scotland by marrying his daughter to the enemy. Margaret Tudor became the Queen of James IV of Scotland. The marriage resulted in a quarrel over the dowry of the princess and the Scots met their worst ever disaster in the Battle of Flodden (1513), where James IV fell along with 'the flower of Scottish chivalry.'

His successor as king, James V, distrusted his uncle Henry VIII and disappointed him by first marrying a daughter of Francis I of France and, on her death, by renewing the French bond in a marriage with Mary of Guise, sister of the Duke of Guise. James V's engagement with the old enemy led to another humiliating defeat by the English army at Solway Moss (1542). The King died shortly after the battle. The heir to the throne was a baby girl, Mary, then just a week old, who would become Mary, Queen of Scots.

The Scots sought to use the crisis for a change of allies and promote the infant Mary in marriage to Henry VIII's son, Edward. Henry favoured the marriage but the plan was nullified by Mary's mother who contrived to take her to France where she remained for thirteen years, receiving education in the dissolute French court. Henry was so angry that he sent an army to ravage Scotland (the 'Rough Wooing'). The fact that the Scots should have desired such a marriage marked a rising dissatisfaction with the long-standing French alliance. Mary of Guise and Mary, Queen of Scots, were destined to make every effort to oppose the trend.

Mary of Guise became Regent of Scotland in 1554 and did everything in her power to maintain French influence in Scotland. The Guise family dominated both French and Scottish courts, but the Lords of the Congregation suspended Mary as Regent in 1559. The presence of French troops allowed her to maintain her hold but when she died on 11 June 1560, her policy of maintaining Roman Catholicism with French help collapsed, thus bringing down both the Roman Church and the 'auld alliance'.

The Reformation in Scotland came to be associated with the reversal of the old alignment with France and the new alignment with England, yet without the subjection of the country to the rule of the Tudors.